Designing and using organizational surveys

DESIGNING AND USING ORGANIZATIONAL SURVEYS

Allan H. Church and
Janine Waclawski

Routledge
Taylor & Francis Group

LONDON AND NEW YORK

First published 1998 by Gower Publishing

2 Park Square, Milton Park, Abingdon, Oxfordshire OX14 4RN
711 Third Avenue, New York, NY 10017, USA

Routledge is an imprint of the Taylor & Francis Group, an informa business

First issued in paperback 2017

British Library Cataloguing in Publication Data
Church, Allan H.
    Designing and using organizational surveys
    1. Employee attitude surveys 2. Employee attitude surveys –
    Methodology
    I.Title II.Waclawski, Janine
    658.3'14'0723

Library of Congress Cataloging-in-Publication Data
Church, Allan H., 1966-
    Designing and using organizational surveys / Allan H. Church,
    Janine Waclawski
        p.   cm.
    Includes bibliographical references and index.
    ISBN 0–566–07975–5 (hardback)
    1. Employee attitude surveys.   I. Waclawski, Janine, 1966-
II. Title.
HF5549.5.A83C48   1998
658.3'14'0723—dc21   98-16696
                                              CIP

Typeset in Century Old Style by Wearset, Boldon, Tyne and Wear

ISBN 13: 978-0-566-07975-7 (hbk)
ISBN 13: 978-1-138-25613-2 (pbk)

Contents

List of figures

List of tables

Acknowledgements

For those of us who are unaccustomed to or uncomfortable with the art of giving praise well, the acknowledgements page is perhaps the most difficult part of a book to write. While this may seem like an exaggeration, it is none the less true. The reason stems in part from not knowing 'the right words' to use when saying thanks. The ability to sum up all of one's feelings of gratitude in a few simple lines takes a combination of eloquence and feeling. To say thank you to a mentor, friend or colleague in a way that sounds both intelligent and genuine is no easy task. With this said, we would like to try and express our appreciation for those who have helped us along the way and hope that our simple words will do them the justice they deserve.

First and foremost, we are especially indebted and grateful to our mentor W. Warner Burke who has been unfailing in his support of us both personally and professionally. Warner, more than any other person, has helped us attain the collective knowledge and experiences which have led to the development of this book. Over the years, he has given us innumerable opportunities to acquire, enhance and refine our skills in the survey arena. Many of the sample survey items examples and anecdotes used throughout the book come from consulting projects we have undertaken in our work with him over the past six years. Without him, this book could not have been written.

We would also like to thank Dale Crossman for suggesting us for this project and to Denis Kinlaw who reviewed our proposal and worked with us on the first draft of our introductory chapter. When Dale first approached us with the idea of submitting a proposal on a survey book we were extremely pleased and excited, though not without some degree of trepidation. Although between us we had over 60 published articles, several book chapters and two doctoral dissertations, this was to be our first book. Fortunately for us, Denis made the process of moving from an initial proposal to an outline an easier one.

Our thanks to the team at Gower Publishing. In particular, we would like to thank our editorial director Malcolm Stern for being so patient with us and our fledgling manuscript. Solveig Gardner Servian the managing editor and Carol

Lucas our copy-editor also deserve thanks for the hard work they put into the final manuscript. Solveig was invaluable in helping us tie up all of the loose ends and manage all of the details necessary to go to print. Carol did an excellent job of copy-editing the document; in addition to all of her work in correcting our grammar and punctuation she also had the somewhat awesome task of helping two Yanks turn American into English.

The many unnamed clients, including those not described in the manuscript, with whom we have worked over the years and from whom we have learned a great deal also deserve our thanks.

Penultimately, we would like to thank our students at Teachers College, Columbia University in class TJ 5018 (aka Data-Based Methods of Organizational Change) for being guinea pigs or more appropriately, sounding boards for much of the material contained in this book. Our students proved to be an invaluable source of feedback (both positive and not so positive), which was so important in shaping the final manuscript. Our students' intellectual curiosity in asking for greater detail and clarity and their probity in giving us feedback about the quality of our content worked together to produce what we believe to be a better book.

Last but not least, we would like to thank our in-house proofreader Mary Zippo for her work in copy-editing the initial drafts of this manuscript. Mary's remarkable ability to read and reread the same chapters over and over again without falling asleep or being driven to physical violence is testament to her professionalism.

Janine Waclawski
Allan H. Church

18 March 1998

Introduction

Welcome to the Information Age. Although we may not like to think of ourselves as a collection of specific data points just waiting to be identified, gathered and quantified in some controlled fashion, in large part that is what we in fact are. Each of us comprises an endless supply of information, from the factual (e.g., date of birth, gender, ethnicity, religious background, education, etc.) to the attitudinal (preferences, dislikes, opinions, etc.). This is how various information systems perceive, understand and ultimately define our existence. Of course, the fact that our databases are continually growing and changing over the course of our life spans makes it all the more difficult to understand us. This process of understanding, however, through information-gathering (labelled as data collection) and interpretation is one of the primary roles of organizations today. For many organizations, these data – i.e., our individual and collective experiences as human beings – are one of the most important sources of information to be harnessed. These data are the basis and lifeblood of such data-gathering enterprises as political polling, television viewing preferences, undergraduate and graduate record examinations, popular opinion polls on current topics, the national census and targeted marketing efforts for various products. Rest assured that if you are watching a particular programme on television any advertisements shown have been targeted at your segment of the marketplace. In today's burgeoning information society understanding the effective use of data collection and interpretation through survey methodology in organizations presents one key means of increasing our understanding of the human experience.

In the organizational context, surveys play an important role in helping leaders and managers obtain a better understanding of the thoughts, feelings, and behaviours of their own employees and of their customers. In fact, surveys are one of the most widely used techniques in contemporary organizations for gathering data from a large number of people in a short amount of time. More than 70 per cent of US organizations today survey their employees either on an annual or at least biannual basis (Paul and Bracken, 1995). The trend towards survey usage appears still to be going up rather than down. For example, while the Mayflower Group – one of the élite survey consortia populated by the top-ranked organizations in their respective industries – contained only 15 charter members at its inception in 1971, the group boasted a membership of 42 in 1995 and a growth rate of 40 per cent since 1985 (Johnson, 1996). Similarly, presentations and research at professional conferences on surveys and their applications have been consistently popular over the years. Moreover, within the 1980s and 1990s, organizational surveys have moved from the sole province of academic (Center for Applied Social Research at Columbia University) and research-based (e.g., the Census Bureau, Gallup, etc.) institutions to either internal organization development (OD) and human resource development (HRD) functions and/or external consulting firms versed in applied research methods.

The popularity of the survey process in organizations can be traced in large part to two main factors:

1. People usually like surveys. They have a broad-based appeal and an implied sense of legitimacy in their usage. And they are viewed by many people as being a democratic, fair and typically confidential means of assessing a wide range of opinions. Although prior experience with poorly implemented organizational surveys may have left some people disillusioned (we will return to this issue in a later section), most people like the idea of being asked their opinions, thoughts and ideas. It is human nature.

2. The ease of use and basic effectiveness of the survey methodology as compared with other approaches for collecting similar types of data – for example, one-to-one interviewing, observations, focus groups, etc. – have not escaped practitioners or those commanding the organizational budgets. Large-scale survey efforts are not typically cheap, but they are considerably less expensive and simultaneously more reliable than any other approach currently available. Furthermore, depending on the use to which the survey effort is directed, the costs may seem trivial when compared with the value of the information obtained.

Despite the inherent popularity and widespread usage of survey methods in organizations today, practitioners are still in need of further guidance regarding how to effectively implement and manage the entire survey process due to the continual growth and evolution of survey processes. It may appear on the surface to be relatively easy to generate some interesting questions and send them out to people to complete; in actuality the survey process is a highly complex and situationally dependent one, in need of careful management. Many factors must be considered before a survey can be used as an *effective* tool for the organization. Some of these include: obtaining the necessary resources and political support to obtain support from the organization, developing questions that appropriately reflect the specific purpose to which the survey effort is directed, the nature and

2

content of the communication process, working through resistance and feed-back, interpreting the survey's results in a meaningful and effective manner and working with those results throughout the organization.

Many good books have been written about the specifics of survey research and its methodology – i.e., sampling schemes, item construction and response theory, multivariate analyses – but, usually, these works have not been designed to provide the organizational practitioner with a clear, concise and pragmatic working guide for how to go about doing a survey. This book is intended to fill that void. In short, our aim is to supply HRD and OD practitioners with an easy-to-use, practical, hands-on guide to conducting successful organizational surveys. In contrast to the more academic resources described above, this book was written primarily for the organizational practitioner who wants help in con-ducting surveys. Therefore, wherever possible, we have made use of real situ-ations and learnings from actual large-scale survey efforts conducted in organizational settings to enhance our points. This book should prove most useful for anyone involved in the use and/or implementation of large-scale organizational surveys – including professionals in human resource manage-ment, organization development, communications, training and development – as well as leaders and managers working with others to implement surveys (or the results of such efforts) in their own organizations.

First, however, let us define what we mean by a survey and the type of surveys to which we will be referring throughout this book.

WHAT IS A SURVEY?

A survey can be loosely defined as any process used for asking people a number of questions (general or specific) to gain information. The information can be either factual, attitudinal or designed to assess an individual's beliefs or judge-ments (Schuman and Kalton, 1985). On the surface, this definition seems gener-ally acceptable. It carries with it basic elements of a survey, and many different types of data collection efforts could be classified as such. For example, a series of telephone interviews conducted in a particular locality asking homeowners about the quality of their refuse collection would be considered a survey under this umbrella, as would a questionnaire distributed at the copy machine regard-ing the quality and reliability of its performance. Some authors would agree with such classifications, but this definition of a survey is far too broad to be consid-ered useful here. As we have already noted, there are many other books that may be suitable for these more general approaches. Rather, given this book's concentration on the HRD and OD practitioner, we have chosen to define our use of the term *organizational survey* as follows: *A systematic process of data collection designed to quantitatively measure specific aspects of organizational members' experience as they relate to work.*

In most cases, this type of organizational survey involves the use of a standardized questionnaire containing a series of items and associated response scales, although such a survey could also be conducted using a telephone (voice-response unit) or even via individual interviews, the latter of which would fundamentally defeat the advantages of the large-scale approach. Aside from the obvious emphasis on organizational members and settings contained in the definition, there are a number of unique elements that should be highlighted for the reader.

First, we are concerned primarily with a *systematic process* for conducting surveys. This is not to say that a simple sample opinion survey could not be quickly thrown together and administered, and yield meaningful findings, because it can. More often than not, however, some important element is missed and the results end up being obtuse or uninterpretable, or the questionnaire will be issued to the wrong sample or even contain the wrong items. Any survey effort, whether large or more moderate in scale, should be taken seriously by those administering it. It certainly will be by those being questioned. This means that some type of planned, systematic approach should be adopted and attention should be paid to effectively managing each of the main phases of the survey process.

It may seem simplistic, but remember that the purpose is *data collection designed to quantitatively measure* something. While we will try not to inflict on the reader all the statistical terminology that normally accompanies such an emphasis, the quality of the specific questions included on the survey document and the manner in which they are displayed and administered have an effect on the quality and quantity of responses returned. For example, the level of detail obtained for a question using a three-point scale (i.e., agree, neutral, disagree) will be vastly different from the same question using a seven-point scale using more gradations in meaning. Sometimes these effects simply offset each other and are worth knowing about only to be informed, but in other cases some simple changes can have a drastic impact on the information received. A case in point: a simple wording change in a survey item from 'generates creative solutions' to 'creates solutions' alters the meaning of the statement completely. Another issue related to data and measurement is emphasis on quantification. More specifically, while survey efforts can contain many different types of questions (e.g., scaled items, write-in comments, forced choice options), fundamentally the value of a large-scale survey effort is that it provides a significant quantity of responses from people on the *exact same question with the exact same response options.* This means that it is relatively easy to interpret, work with and analyse

4

the data collected assuming the question itself was clear at the start. To sum it all up, there is an old adage in the survey (and consulting business) that says – 'You get what you measure' or, more crudely put, 'Garbage in, garbage out'. In the application of organizational surveys, these sayings hold true as well.

The phrase *specific aspects of organizational members' experience* in the definition above refers to the type of information or data ultimately to be collected. This comes back to the very purpose of the survey effort itself. The following list of potential content areas highlight the different topics that can be assessed in a survey:

- Are you interested in knowing if employees feel empowered in their jobs?
- Do you want to know which types of communication systems are most and least effective for communicating different types of messages?
- Are managers behaving in ways that reinforce the new mission and vision of the organization?
- How satisfied are employees in their jobs?
- What are the barriers to enhancing employees' performance?
- Do employees at all levels of the organization understand and commit to the stated mission or vision of the company?
- What are employees' perceptions about compensation and benefits?
- Do employees think that organizational changes are occurring too quickly or not quickly enough?
- Is the current organization structure one that facilitates the completion of work?
- What is the perception of the organization's senior leadership team?

This list contains only a small sample of the types of questions that can be included in an organizational survey. The potential list is limitless and, in fact, is only constrained by the experience (e.g., content knowledge, background, formal education, prior work with surveys, etc.) of the survey developer and the scope of the project.

We will discuss the aspect of identifying one's survey objectives in the first chapter, the message here is that those people behind the survey effort need to be clear about (a) what kind of information they want, (b) how they want to assess it using a questionnaire methodology, and (c) what they intend to do with that information when it has been collected. All this has a significant bearing on the specific aspects of the survey.

Based on just this brief list of possible topics for an organizational survey, it should be clear to the reader that surveys, even as we have defined them here, can serve a multitude of purposes in organizations. This is due, in large part, to the variety of sources from which our contemporary approach to conducting and using surveys developed. The following section provides a brief history of these

5

sources and influences, followed by a more detailed discussion of the general uses of organizational surveys in contemporary organizational life.

A BRIEF HISTORY OF SURVEYS

Given the popularity and widespread use of surveys in most organizations today, it may be surprising for some people to note that surveys (as we know them) were not used extensively in organizations until the post-Second World War era. The actual application of surveys for assessing employees' thoughts and opinions, which seems quite straightforward and natural today, actually evolved as an offshoot of a variety of factors, which we discuss below. Until relatively recently, however, survey techniques and usage resided primarily within the academic, military and political realms. Nevertheless, the basic premise of surveys or, more specifically, survey methodology has existed for a very long time. In fact, if we consider the more general survey definition previously discussed – i.e., *A survey is any process used for asking people a number of questions (general or specific) to gain information* – it is apparent that surveys have existed since the beginnings of formal language. The first recorded use of surveys, for example, dates back to the ancient Egyptians who are credited with the establishment of the census process for simply counting the number of inhabitants (Babbie, 1973). We also know that the Romans used crude survey techniques to find out how many people and of what types lived in their great cities.

Despite its ancient heritage, the survey as a formal methodological approach for collecting data in organizations did not gain widespread acceptance until the 1950s. One of the most significant contributors to the contemporary use of survey feedback is the early and ground-breaking work by researchers such as Samuel Stouffer and Paul Lazarsfeld. Their efforts are generally credited for the acceptance, popularity and, above all, quality of surveys today (Babbie, 1973; Higgs and Ashworth, 1996). These researchers concentrated on developing and refining survey methods and analyses to improve empiricism in the social sciences. Their contribution to the field today can be traced to their use of survey methods to examine significant social issues of the time, such as the effects of the Great Depression on people's well-being, the status of Blacks in the 1930s, the effects of McCarthyism, and the effects of social factors on the formal presidential voting process. These individuals examined various social, political and economic factors in America using a large-scale survey technique. Lazarsfeld is also credited with establishing the first academic centre for survey research – the Bureau for Applied Social Research at Columbia University (Babbie, 1973).

Surveys have been used throughout the development of western civilization to gather many different types of information, from people's socio-economic status,

6

Table 0.1 Different types of survey data

Political	Economic	Social
• public opinion polling	• census	• attitudes and opinions
• voting processes	• market/product research	• leadership
• election polling	• advertising testing	• religious values
• party affiliation	• economic behaviour	• social issues
• census		

annual income, and place of residence to their opinions about political leaders, religion, capital punishment and consumer preferences. Before gaining prominence and widespread exposure in organizations these tools were used extensively (and still are, for that matter) in three different arenas: political, economic and social. Table 0.1 shows a breakdown of the different types of survey data collected that reflect common emphases and applications for each of these three domains.

Many of these types of surveys are still commonly used today. For example, the USA's election process (at the city, state and federal levels) is in fact a *very* large-scale survey. Most of the population are eligible to vote but, generally, only a certain sample will participate (by vote) in the election of a given representative. This response set or sample is then used to determine which official will represent the entire population. Furthermore, at the federal level, the construction of the Electoral College mandates that each state receive a certain number of electoral votes, depending on the size of its population (based on census data). Similarly, many business organizations, such as IBM, have extensive research functions, with literally hundreds of professionals devoted to the sole purpose of surveying and analysing market trends among current users and potential buyers of their products. Collecting data on people's responses to new advertising campaigns is also a common practice among such organizations, particularly given the exorbitant costs associated with running such spots on national television and in popular magazines and newspapers. Last but not least, the social sciences are anything but inactive in the area of current survey usage, both with respect to examining social issues – i.e., the province of many sociologists – as well as various organizational and related social psychological applications.

CONTEMPORARY GROWTH AND USAGE OF SURVEYS

These days there are a number of organizations that base their entire existence on their survey practice. A. C. Nielson and Arbitron, for example, are two of the largest private sector survey firms that use surveys to estimate television viewing audiences (Rossi, Wright and Anderson, 1983). Similarly, academic institutions such as the National Opinion Research Center (NORC), as well as popular media surveys like the CBS–New York Times poll and the Gallup Organization, have done a great deal to promote surveys in the eyes of the general public. There are many management and organization consulting firms today that specialize specifically in conducting and/or providing advice regarding organizations' surveys, many of which have been founded or are populated by HRD and OD professionals who have left their internal positions in survey departments in the past.

Many factors have served to increase the acceptance and usage of employee survey approaches in the world, but the birth of the Mayflower Group, a consortium of 42 blue-chip companies, in 1971 (Johnson, 1996) marked perhaps the most significant turning-point in the history of organizational survey research. This professional group was developed specifically to advance the practice of opinion surveying in organizations by sharing best practices and normative data among firms. This highly unusual (in the business world at least) process of sharing information has led to the establishment and maintenance of a database for bench-marking purposes across organizations. The formation and continued existence of this consortium has shown the willingness of, and trust, required for companies to exchange potentially sensitive information, which is a positive trend given the continued competitiveness of the world marketplace. The participation of highly profitable and well-respected companies such as IBM, Sears, Xerox, 3M, Merck, Johnson & Johnson, GTE and DuPont, just to name a few, not only demonstrates the importance attached to survey research in top-tier organizations but also serves to place a seal of approval on the survey process in general. It also sets an example for other companies to follow. Surveys, both in and out of organizations, are here to stay.

SURVEYS IN CONTEMPORARY ORGANIZATIONAL LIFE

But why do surveys continue to be so popular in organizations? One of the likely reasons for survey usage is the diversity of applications to which the results and even the process of a survey effort can be directed. For the HRD and OD practitioner, surveys provide a myriad of possible uses and can sometimes simultaneously serve a number of different objectives. Some of the more significant categories of uses include:

- to understand and explore employee opinions and attitudes
- to provide a general and/or a specific assessment of the behaviours and attributes inherent in employees' day-to-day work experience
- to create baseline measures and use these for bench-marking various behaviours, processes and other aspects of organizations against other either internal or external measures
- to use the data for driving organizational change and development.

Each of these applications will be described in greater detail below. It should be noted before continuing, however, that these categories are not mutually exclusive. In fact, survey efforts usually involve a combination of these different objectives.

Traditionally, and in their early use in organizations, surveys had been concentrated on assessing the opinions, attitudes and beliefs of organizational members. Early applications of this approach involved attempts to gauge workers' knowledge of and interest in potential unionization efforts, among other topics, but more contemporary examples of this type of objective include measuring such individual and personal beliefs and feelings as employee satisfaction, empowerment, organizational commitment, autonomy, work–life balance, pride in the company and perceptions of fairness and equity in standardized policies, systems and procedures. Other types of questionnaires have been designed to measure more involved and detailed topics such as rankings of which employee assistance programmes would be most desirable (given a list of types from which to choose), opinions of the quality of training and development efforts and programmes, reactions to various messages and strategic initiatives, and external perceptions direct from the customer or client of product service or quality. All these types of data can be extremely useful for planning at every level, from the senior most strategic perspective to the extremely tactical implementation of a compensation and benefits programme at a local department level. The one caveat with the measurement of employee opinions which can be held against the use of any type of survey but that is particularly poignant here, is that one needs to *be prepared to openly acknowledge and ultimately attempt to deal with the issues raised.* One of the most difficult problems that surveys administrators often face is finding a 'bad' outcome on an important item – e.g., employee motivation or morale – only to realize that no one in HR or senior management for that matter wants to actually take up the issue with employees. This 'duck and cover' approach to dealing with survey findings often results in the alignment of many negative forces against current and future survey efforts that might be undertaken.

A second type of survey objective concerns the assessment or measurement of more specific behaviours and conditions that exist in organizational life. Most survey efforts are often a combination of this and the opinion approach; however, assessment surveys differ in that they involve identifying certain observable behavioural tendencies that can be accurately rated by employees. Since the assessment of behaviour involves the observation of various individuals engaging in these behaviours or actions, this type of assessment typically involves questions pertaining to the actions of immediate managers, functional, divisional or business unit managers, and senior managers and executives. We will discuss the details of developing and using different types of items in more detail in a later chapter, but some sample items of this nature are listed below:

Please rate the extent to which …
- senior management is consistent in word and deed
- senior management communicates with employees at all levels
- your manager awards and recognizes people in your work unit
- your manager provides you with the information you need to do your job.

These types of data are intended to provide more specific and actionable information than the opinion perspective alone. Attitudes and opinions are helpful; however, they are not as easy to act on at the individual level. You cannot say to a manager, for example, 'Make your employees feel more satisfied' without knowing what conditions will lead to employee satisfaction. Through the use of surveys and data analysis, one can identify what types of specific behaviours or working conditions need to be changed or reinforced, which will ultimately lead to that employee feeling more satisfied. This is a somewhat subtle distinction, but very important none the less. In many ways, these two types of survey objectives represent the distinction between a survey that simply 'captures a picture of the present state' and one that can be used for diagnosing and effecting significant organizational change.

Another popular use and objective of survey methodology is its contribution to the 'bench-marking' process. Bench-marking is a means of comparing survey results from one's own organization with some predetermined measure or bench mark to identify relative strengths and weaknesses. Many practitioners think of bench-marking in terms of external indicators, but it is also quite acceptable to use survey data as an internal bench mark, both with respect to other functions, divisions and work processes at the same point in time as well as over time. In its simplest form, for example, a company can use an initial effort to establish a baseline measure against which future survey results can be tracked. Therefore, a bench-marking survey can be used to assess improvement or decline over time on the specific areas it has been designed to measure. Similarly, by incorporating a range of responses for the highest and lowest performing units (e.g., departments or work teams) suitable for comparison with the present level of results, the survey client can gain an immediate understanding of the areas in which he or she excels relative to the rest of the organization and those which could benefit from additional support and learning through the exchange of best practices from within. In addition to internal bench-marking, many organizational members are also interested in knowing how their individual and collective data compare with other organizations. These external indicators can range from the most competitive firms within their own industry to companies in entirely different industries but with similar types of processes or those facing similar issues. When using competitors within the same industry for bench-marking purposes, survey clients are typically interested in knowing how they rate with respect to their competition on certain areas of organizational functioning. In other words, they want to know how they rate against the competition in the areas that they feel are necessary for success. When using organizations in different industries as a point of comparison, the purpose is often to see how one's own company fares outside of its industry as an indication of its overall competitiveness, irrespective of industry type. Given the increasing tendency for organizations to span national boundaries and compete in different markets, this approach has more credibility than perhaps it once did. The previously mentioned Mayflower Group represents one such type of comparison. Members in this group receive norms on a number of standard items classified both by and across industry type.

Perhaps of most concern to HRD and OD practitioners is the use of organizational surveys for the express purposes of organizational change and development. Practitioners have long acknowledged that databased feedback is one of the most powerful means for effecting change (Nadler, 1977) and recent studies based on individualized multirater feedback methods have supported this contention (Atwater and Yammarino, 1992; Church, 1994a, 1997; Church and Bracken, 1997; Church and Waclawski, 1997; Van Velsor, Taylor and Leslie, 1993). During the 1990s, the use of survey data for organizational change has become increasingly popular and a number of external consulting firms have begun to specialize in these services. The basis of the questions themselves are often similar to or the same as those described above; however, there is a fundamental difference in this approach in that the survey process is seen as only a part of a larger change initiative involving other complementary methods. Furthermore, the survey questionnaire itself is seen as both *a means of communicating what is important to the organization*, particularly if some aspect of behaviour change or a change in strategic direction is required, and *a way to identify, link, and leverage key variables that lead to desired end-states in the organization* (such as increased morale) to those that actually cause or drive them. This type of analysis, although complex to conduct and interpret, represents

11

perhaps the most powerful and potentially effective application of survey results. In effect, individual opinions and assessments of workers' behaviours are used to identify and drive those organizational changes that will have the greatest impact on future behaviour and success. Surveys, if concentrated on this objective, can provide HRD practitioners and organizational leadership with important information about employees' perceptions about change and their readiness for it, as well as many other issues that can affect the success or failure of large-scale change initiatives (Church, Margiloff and Coruzzi, 1995; Waclawski, 1996a).

THE SEVEN STEPS TO EFFECTIVE ORGANIZATIONAL SURVEYS

If we have made our point so far, it should be clear that while almost anyone can participate in a survey effort, there are a number of significant issues and complexities that need to be managed if the outcome is to be a positive one. In the following text you will be introduced to the seven steps, or phases, involved in implementing an organizational survey. Figure 0.1 shows the stages. Below is an overview of what each of the steps entails.

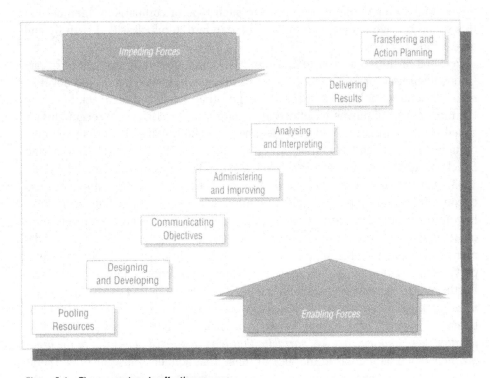

Figure 0.1   The seven steps to effective surveys

Step 1 focuses on the process of 'Pooling resources' in the early stages of a survey. As in any sizeable organizational initiative or intervention, one must always begin by laying the appropriate groundwork with all the right people. Gaining substantive input and co-operation from all key parties in the organization is never an easy task, and without the appropriate support and resources most survey efforts will fall short of expectations with respect to impact. In order to satisfy the needs of important constituencies and the ultimate end-users of the survey, involvement early on is crucial. In this section we will discuss the elements involved in setting the stages for a successful organizational survey effort. This includes how to set clear strategic objectives regarding the purpose and uses of the survey process itself; how to obtain commitment from senior management as well as the rank and file of the organization; how to identify and overcome negative energy and/or apathy due to prior experiences; who should be involved in the data collection effort and what specific types of information are to be collected; what types of additional information (e.g., demographics and/or organizational characteristics, etc.) should be collected and at what levels; and how to prepare the organization for the survey effort. This first stage in the survey process comprises building alliances, support, commitment and energy for the survey effort before it can really begin. In our experience it is this stage, more than any other, that will determine the ultimate success or failure of the survey effort with respect to its perceived viability as a worthwhile endeavour. In other words, organizational initiatives are often judged (be it fairly or not) by those people who stand behind them and those who do not.

Step 2 concentrates on the second stage in the survey process – i.e., the fundamentals of the survey instrumentation itself. In 'Developing a world-class survey' we will look at characteristics of the questions themselves, the content, the response options and scales, the layout or presentation and the formal instructions, to name a few. After a brief comparison of the pros and cons of using existing standardized instruments from other sources versus creating a customized survey tool, the section will turn to the issue of design. Through examples and descriptions of prior research and experience, the survey practitioner will be guided on the importance of using teamwork to build high-quality surveys instruments; gathering, identifying and working through key issues that need to be assessed; drafting a survey instrument; and pre-testing and refining it for final administration. By the end of this section, practitioners should have a better understanding of how to write items that (a) concentrate on specific issues, (b) are clear and easy to respond to, (c) avert the typical problems often found in new questionnaires, (d) are free of jargon and cultural biases, (e) are methodologically sound, and (f) are appropriate for the level and type of readership at which they are directed. The issue of response options or scales will also be dealt with in detail, as will the pros and cons of using write-in comments to help augment and add spice to the more quantitative data collected. The use of frameworks, models or organizing themes for the survey instrument to enhance respondent's understanding of, and interest in, completion of the survey will also be discussed, as will the benefits of exploring potential linkages ahead of time with other existing (or impending) organizational measurement and/or change initiatives.

In Step 3, we turn our attention to one of the most simple to understand yet difficult to implement concepts inherent in the survey process – communication. In 'Communicating objectives' we start with another old adage, which says 'communicate, communicate, communicate'. Many practitioners, managers and leaders for that matter would agree with this sentiment, but few in our experience actually follow through with this edict. And yet it is one of the basic aspects of an effective survey process. In this chapter we look at the importance of communicating the purpose, objectives and content of the survey initiative clearly and effectively to those involved in the data collection effort (i.e., the employees completing the survey). Of course, this means gaining agreement first among those in power as to what are the expected outcomes of the survey effort. It also means laying the necessary groundwork to ensure that people are in agreement with the survey's objectives and that they understand how the data is intended to be used and the issues of confidentiality. Thus, after a brief introduction and overview of the contents, processes, roles (CPR) model of organizational communication as a means for understanding the issues inherent in organizational communication, this section will explore each of the phases of communication in a survey effort from first contact to the formal information provided with the survey instrument. General guidelines for communicating to employees, strengths and weaknesses of various mechanisms for sending messages, and the need to balance the amount of information given so that it is neither too much nor too little will all be discussed. Also covered is the need to manage the informal communication system – i.e., the grapevine. In some organizations, this can be a more powerful means of making or breaking a survey than anything the senior leadership or even the immediate manager says. Besides these larger issues, the covering letter itself and accompanying instructions on the instrument (i.e., how all these messages come together for the respondents) will also be discussed in this section. One should always remember that although clear communication in and of itself will not save a bad survey effort, poor communication can kill a good one.

Step 4 covers what is for some the most mundane and for others the most stressful part of the survey effort: the formal administration process. In 'Administering the survey' we will discuss the details involved in carrying off a successful administration. This includes everything from the importance of establishing a clear, comprehensive and, above all, reasonable project plan with appropriate milestones, checkpoints and buffer areas for making up lost time when dates begin to slide, as they invariably do, to holding your internal or external clients' hands and allaying their fears and concerns regarding the process and the inevitable glitches that occur. Also covered will be the specific methods of, and options for, the administration itself. For example, what are the pros and cons of mailing the survey to each individual employee with return envelopes versus having mass administration sessions in large auditoriums with proctors? Who should complete the survey first? What types of data collection methods should be used? Organizational surveys typically conjure images of paper and pencil questionnaires with optical scan response forms, but with the advent of the Information Age there are now a variety of other alternatives for collecting survey data. Some of these include computers that gather the information via keys you press over the telephone (also known as voice-response units), individual computer disk-based methods in which you respond to the survey on your own computer and then return the disk to someone else for processing, or even e-mail response options (Kuhnert and McCauley, 1996). These alternatives are often very exciting, particularly to those who are either enamoured of computer technology or who are bored with the more tried and traditional methods, and they all have their respective strengths and weaknesses, which we highlight where appropriate, that can impact their effectiveness and usefulness in various situations. Pencil and paper methods remain the most commonly used in organizations, for reasons which will become clear in our discussion. Step 4 will also cover the importance of having a continuous learning and process improvement orientation to working with surveys in organizations. This involves making effective use of feedback from the organization, particularly in the early stages of administration, to adjust and adapt the process to make it optimally effective in a given situation.

Next, in Step 5, 'Interpreting results', we move to one of the most potentially complex and subsequently misunderstood aspects of survey work. Once all the data have been collected, it is time to put it into that 'black box', as our clients sometimes call it, and analyse the results. Most people, and especially those individuals with advanced degrees, can calculate an average value from a series of responses collected in a survey effort, without having done a good deal of previous survey work or without having experience in applied research on large-scale data sets, but it is a much more difficult and refined skill to be able to pull all of the results together into a cohesive yet simultaneously statistically supported story about what is occurring in the organization. There are always arguably many different stories and themes that result from any survey effort that spans a large population of people, but we are concerned here primarily with the first wave of analysis – i.e., the one that is presented first to the survey client and/or the senior management organization (other types of subsequent analytic work will be discussed in Step 6). Such an effort requires the practitioner to identify the main issues and important relationships among a mass of data in what is also often the shortest time frame of the entire survey effort. This is because once the survey has been sent out and people start responding, everyone wants to know the results as soon as possible. It can take five months to develop the appropriate questions for use in the questionnaire itself, the time from final data collection to the first reporting process must be only a matter of a few short weeks for the results to be meaningful and have the appropriate credibility upon which to take action. Time and time again we have seen a senior management team receive their initial top-level results (i.e., the 'big picture') shortly after final administration, only to be so disturbed by the findings of the questions they asked that we literally withhold the feedback from employees for several months, making the results far less relevant and lacking in impact when they were finally communicated (not to mention the impact such actions have on the credibility and utility of future survey efforts). In this section we will discuss such topics as how to make a compelling story of a large collection of numbers with and without advanced statistics, how to balance expectations with realities inherent in the data, how to work with normative and bench-marking data to assist in interpreting the results rather than becoming the focal point, and how to use write-in comments to enrich the data and presentation. The uses and abuses of the bench-marking process will be discussed in greater detail in this section as well.

Step 6 is concerned with the actual delivery of the survey results to organizational members both in various forms and throughout different levels. In 'Delivering the findings' the emphasis is on picking a strategy for delivering the feedback to all those involved in the organization. This strategy, often described as a 'roll-out process', is conducted on a gradual management-level-by-management-level basis. In some ways this stage also represents the second half of the analysis process whereby the data are re-examined at lower levels and for specific groups, functions, departments, comparisons or segments to look among similar or different stories in their specific findings. For example, in a large-scale organizational survey it is possible not only to provide reports for every department with a certain number of people responding, but also to provide a report that compares how several different departments rated one another on service quality and co-operation internally. A simple presentation of results can easily be undertaken without the benefit of subsequent interpretation, but to maximize effectiveness the roll-out process should involve some degree of interpretative assistance built into the framework of the delivery vehicle itself. Of course, the specific timing as well as the complexity of the information delivered must also be carefully managed for the results to be meaningful. Just as waiting too long to provide any feedback is problematic, so too is 'dumping' the entire results of the survey on all employees in some overly complex and underinterpreted fashion so that no one can understand what it all means, which by the way we have seen in some organizations in well intentioned but misconstrued attempts to be entirely open in their survey communications. Other issues with respect to feedback delivery to be covered in this section include tips for making formal presentations have an impact, using organizational models and frameworks for describing linkages or relationships among key variables of interest, resisting when requests for additional data threaten the ethical integrity of the confidentiality norms established at the outset of the survey process, and how to present good and not so good data in ways that recipients can accept.

Finally, Step 7 centres on the last stage of the survey process: 'Learning into action'. Many clients and practitioners pay little attention to this phase once they reach it, feeling instead that now that the survey is done and all the feedback delivered it can just be forgotten. The fact is that this stage can make or break the survey effort. Even the best planning, the most well-constructed questionnaire, a solid administration process, strong analysis and a variety of staged feedback reports will not be enough to make a survey effort effective to the organization if the data are not used to drive change and improvements in the system or in people's day-to-day behaviours. Thus, in this chapter we discuss the importance of follow-through. Regardless of the objectives of the survey effort itself (e.g., to gauge employee opinion, to assess behavioural tendencies, to communicate and reinforce the culture, to target areas for change and development initiatives), it is of paramount importance that the results be used by recipients to make decisions and take actions that will ultimately affect the organization's future. We are concerned here with issues of action planning, identifying areas for intervention and improvement, enlisting and involving others in the process, measuring progress over time through resurvey efforts and linking survey results to other key measures of organizational performance. If the organization does not take ownership of the results, the data will have no meaning and therefore no impact. This occurs with many surveys in today's organizations. It can also happen to new survey efforts that fail to receive adequate support from senior management and other key opinion leaders in the organization at the outset, and these efforts become lame ducks. It can also happen to those survey systems that have been in place for years, where engaging in the survey has created a routine process that employees do not trust, respect or pay attention to, but is none the less used by management as a 'dipstick' for gauging employee opinion. Step 7 describes how to prevent this type of entropy in the survey process.

17

1 Pooling resources

Silence is the most perfect expression of scorn.

George Bernard Shaw

Two of the most important components of an effective organizational survey effort are involvement in and commitment to the process. Many senior managers (and some human resources and organization development personnel as well) would like to believe that conducting a survey is a relatively simple task and therefore should not require much effort beyond deciding what to ask people. However, the fact is that if a survey has not been (a) endorsed by organizational members early in its implementation and (b) integrated and linked into the existing framework of corporate initiatives and directives, it will fail to make a significant impact. This means that very early in the life of the survey effort, as with any large-scale organizational initiative, an appropriate level of support must be obtained from key players in the organizational hierarchy. Because these individuals need to be highly visible and strategically placed, they are typically either senior level managers or high-potential employees being groomed for future leadership positions. Often labelled as champions (Ulrich, 1997) of a given initiative, these proponents serve three necessary functions with respect to the survey process and can help establish the groundwork for building commitment and involvement. A survey champion provides:

- direction and leadership regarding the importance of the survey effort to the larger organizational system and its relationship to existing core business initiatives
- resources in terms of staff, time, and money to support the various phases and aspects of implementation (e.g., development, administration, analysis, integration, action planning and follow-up improvement interventions)
- validity, credibility and significance to the entire survey process for all organizational members.

The first stage in designing and implementing a world-class survey process –

19

i.e., pooling intellectual and political resources – is centred on two subprocesses: (a) identifying the primary objectives and integrating framework of the survey effort and (b) building the alliances, support, commitment, and energy among people in the organization needed to support the successful attainment of these objectives. Once again, while it may seem like a simple and obvious idea that this type of large-scale intervention needs to be grounded in the broader strategic fabric of the organization and receive visible and vocal support from key players to be truly effective, it is none the less an idea that is often overlooked. Many organizations attempt to pursue a survey effort because of the vision of a small group of individuals in the organization development or human resources function (and even with the backing of the most senior human resources person in the organization) only to have the entire project put on hold by top management in anticipation of a more 'appropriate' time to conduct a survey. In other cases, the survey project may move forward but ends up being forced on the organization without the proper alignments and support and, therefore, is doomed to have little or no (or perhaps even negative) impact in the long run.

A significant amount of groundwork with respect to relationship building and strategic integration is needed at the start of any such survey effort, regardless of whether the survey is intended to be used as a one-off diagnostic tool or an annual system for organization development and improvement. For the survey to be perceived by organizational members as an effective mechanism (and 'perceiving is believing' with respect to this type of initiative), it must be built into *and* around the existing organizational reality. Organizations are indeed social systems comprising many different interdependent components (Katz and Kahn, 1978); this means that in order to affect change in one area, other areas must be considered and/or changed as well. A survey conducted without concern for other variables in the organizational system is likely to produce only isolated and limited results.

The Burke–Litwin (B–L) model of organizational change and performance (Burke and Litwin, 1992) provides a good example of how such interdependencies operate (see Figure 1.1). Figure 1.1 shows that from a systemic perspective the higher-level factors of senior leadership, the overall culture and the mission and strategy of the entire company exert a driving force on the day-to-day behaviours of managers, the formal organizational structure and its operating systems (e.g., rewards, communication, selection, promotion, training, etc.). These factors, in turn, affect people's experience in their jobs with respect to the climate in their work group, levels of individual motivation, and the extent to which needs and values and task requirements are met. The reader is directed elsewhere (e.g., Burke, Coruzzi and Church, 1996; Burke and Litwin, 1992) for a more complete discussion of the B–L model for organizational diagnosis and intervention planning. No single facet of organizational existence exists alone.

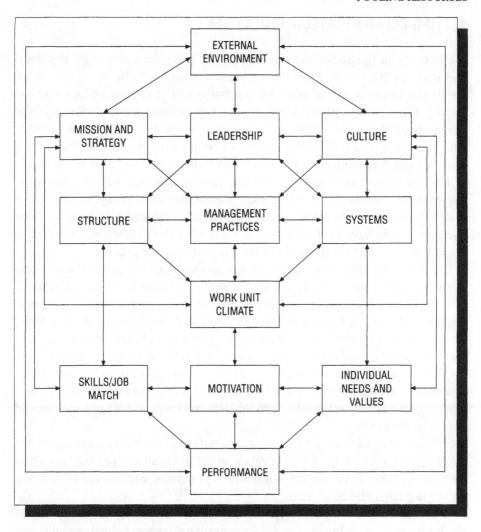

Figure 1.1 The Burke–Litwin model of organizational performance and change
Source: Burke and Litwin (1992), p. 538.

The interrelationships and interdependencies among people, systems and initiatives must be considered when planning a world-class survey process. With this in mind, the remainder of this section will explore how to set clear and strategic objectives for the survey, how to involve organizational members in the process and thereby generate support and commitment, and how to work through apathy and negative attitudes and prepare the organization for the survey roll-out. In short, this step concentrates on how to ensure that the survey does indeed become a fully integrated initiative.

21

SETTING CLEAR STRATEGIC OBJECTIVES

We know from the social and organizational change literature (e.g., Beckhard and Harris, 1987; Lewin, 1958) that an important early step in any change initiative is the identification of expected outcomes or the desired end-state of the process. This is the driving force behind the increasing popularity of future search (e.g., Weisbord, 1995) and whole system methodologies (e.g., Bunker and Alban, 1997), wherein large groups of people are brought together in real time to build commitment to a shared vision of the future and a means to obtain it. For any large-scale initiative including an organizational survey effort to be successful it must have a set of clear and measurable objectives that have immediate relevance and are linked strategically to the organization as a whole. Once these outcomes have been established, the means (and obstacles) by which to achieve them can be identified for those implementing the process.

It is like embarking on a journey. Before you start out you must choose a final destination. You can certainly just start travelling without an end-point in mind, but you will not know where you are going until you get there, and it may turn out that when you do finally arrive it is not a pleasant place to visit after all. Thus, having identified a desired destination for your trip, in order to find your way there you need a road-map, a guidebook, or at least a plan for how to obtain the necessary directions as you get closer. It can be very frustrating to know where you want to go but to have no idea of how to get there. There also needs to be a marker or a signpost at the other end that lets you know when you have reached your final destination.

Following this analogy, if we consider the survey as a means for getting where we are going, then we need first to establish the destination – i.e., the core statement of purpose of the survey – a simple yet pointed explanation of why the survey is going to be conducted.

At first glance this may seem like a very clear-cut and straightforward thing to do, however, as with many complex organizational issues, hidden agendas and political issues can become part of the process (see Figure 1.2). The impact of these fixed factors can be minimized or sometimes even used to enhance the total process if the goals and objectives of the survey are clearly and formally stated, and agreed upon by all constituents involved. This, of course, is why the question of 'who are the key constituents?' becomes important as well.

We have seen these political issues at work many times in organizations and in many different ways. One poignant instance occurred, for example, in an employee opinion survey effort conducted in a large financial services organization following a multiple post-acquisition situation. This organization had in the previous year acquired at least half a dozen smaller competitors in an attempt to consolidate its position in the marketplace as the local retailer of choice for its

22

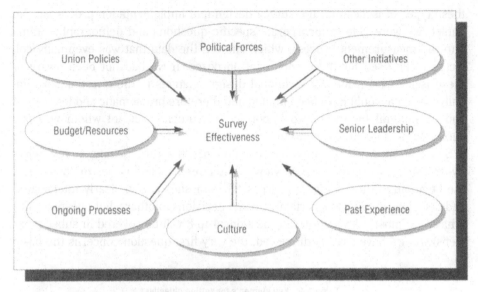

Figure 1.2 Fixed factors influencing survey effectiveness

services. From the point of view of our client, the vice-president of human resources, the formal objectives of the survey itself were to (a) assess the general state of morale in the organization as a result of the recent changes, (b) examine the extent of differences inherent in those employees who had been acquired from various sources versus those who had been with the company prior to these actions, (c) use the results for follow-up organization improvement initiatives and (d) establish a baseline for future assessments. After several meetings with various internal constituent groups, including the second-in-command of the organization and the chair of the organization's diversity committee, it became apparent that the survey was intended to serve other purposes as well. For the second-in-command, who was championing the effort and serving as a figurehead in the organization, the survey would provide a means of communicating his new agenda and interest in employees in preparation for his impending move into the chief executive officer (CEO) position the following year. He intended to use the results to drive his changes, many of which had already been planned in advance, through the organization. The chair of the diversity committee, on the other hand, was interested in exploring trends in employee attitudes and perceptions by various subgroups related to his agenda such as gender, ethnicity, religion, age, marital status, single parent responsibilities, etc. He intended to use the results in order to secure funding and support for various diversity programmes and objectives. By uncovering, exploring and integrating

23

these types of issues into the survey design and implementation process at the outset, we were able to incorporate specific questions and demographic items into the measurement process, which allowed the data that was eventually collected to be used for these additional purposes. If we had not been aware of these issues and made the additional design changes in the questionnaire initially, the data would have been limited and therefore problematic and less useful and meaningful for these two important constituents, one of whom was our survey champion in the organization.

So, what are the most important components of setting quality survey objectives? Table 1.1 provides an overview of the questions and issues to consider at the beginning of the planning process. These issues are all clearly interrelated and decisions in one most certainly impact decisions in others, but questions 1 to 3 have the most relevance here (questions 4 to 8 will be covered in subsequent steps). As we have already discussed, the very first question concerns the basic

Table 1.1 Key elements for setting objectives

1. What is the purpose of the survey?
    Measuring organizational change.
    Measuring employee satisfaction.
    Measuring workplace conditions.

2. What are the expected outcomes of the survey?
    Managing change.
    Improving employee satisfaction.
    Improving performance.

3. Who will be involved in the survey?
    Respondents.
    Item designers.
    Task forces.
    Groups in the organization that will be involved.
    Groups in the organization that will not be involved.

4. What will be the content of the survey?

5. How and when will the data be collected?
    Paper and pencil.
    Voice-response unit.
    On-line.

6. What will the final reports look like?
    At what level will the data be cut?

7. How will the data be reported out and by whom?

8. What steps will be taken as a result of the survey?
    Who will take them?
    When will they be taken?
    How will we measure progress?

purpose of the survey itself. Simply put, why do you want to do a survey? Is it intended to assess the degree of change towards some future state? Are you concerned with employee attitudes, opinions and morale? Is it an exploratory process designed to identify areas for improvement? Do you want to find out how well the various internal communication systems are working and whether employees understand and/or believe the messages provided? Is it meant to communicate a new set of values or behaviours that are important to the future success of organization? These are the kinds of questions that need to be answered. A sample purpose statement provided to employees in a covering letter from senior management in a recent survey effort centred around a corporate initiative as follows:

> The purpose of the enclosed questionnaire is to enable us to measure our progress, at least in the eyes of our people, and to improve our effectiveness towards achieving our goal of improving customer service. Every employee throughout the company is being asked to participate; therefore, for equal representation from all areas, your input is especially valuable.
>
> We are initiating this survey to develop a picture of how employees view the company. In answering these questions, please focus on the company as you experience it in your day-to-day work life. The results are intended to give a broad measure of how we are doing in key areas of mission accomplishment, leadership and management practices, work group performance, and employee satisfaction and effectiveness. To be the best, we must have a unified vision of where we want to be, and a strategy for how to get there. This is especially true in the difficult area of providing improved service to customers.

Once the purpose and objectives of the survey are clear, the question of anticipated outcomes and who should be involved in the process should follow naturally. If the survey is intended only to be used as a static measure, for example, regarding progress towards some change effort (e.g., to become more customer focused), then the outcome of the survey process (but, of course, not the larger change process) may simply be the presentation of the survey results to those groups involved. On the other hand, if the survey is designed to become an integral part of the overall organization development function, then the desired outcomes might reflect, for example, significant improvements over time in employee working conditions, attitudes and morale.

As to who should be involved in the planning and design process, besides the very basic guideline of including some representation from line and staff personnel, the best approach is usually one where a survey task force is formed that represents a broad cross-section of employees from different levels, functions and backgrounds. In this way, the survey objectives, outcomes, content and even implementation strategy can be designed with input from a variety of opinions and perspectives.

As with most complex organizational activities, the clarification and objective-

25

setting process can be an easy and quick one, or it can be a very arduous and time-consuming task. In large part, the level of effort required in this area depends on (a) the number of people involved, and (b) the degree of similarity in expectations among decision-makers. Setting objectives for surveys when done for a single client or a small homogenous group can be achieved with relative speed and ease. If the goals of the survey are limited enough in scope to be well matched to such a small group of planners and implementers, then the effort will likely proceed smoothly. Conversely, the objective-setting process can quickly become unwieldy as the number of constituents and decision-makers increases in size and diversity of opinion. When multiple parties are involved who have different (and often competing) objectives, setting the groundrules may require the assistance of someone with good process consultation (Schein, 1988), group facilitation and conflict management skills.

It all comes back to the issue of effective contracting. From the realm of organizational consultation (e.g., Block, 1981) we know that good contracting at the beginning of any effort, including an organizational survey, can prevent a significant amount of aggravation and disappointment at a later date. In fact, there is no substitute for good contracting with the client, whether that client is external or internal. What we have been talking about all along – i.e., setting clear, measurable and strategic survey objectives – is really part and parcel of establishing a solid survey contract with your client, that is, the survey owner and sponsor. When undertaking a survey initiative set clear expectations and objectives at the outset. This means actively seeking input from key decision-makers about their specific purpose(s) for the conduct of the survey and the desired end state they hope to achieve through its conduct. It also means identifying the specific goals, roles and processes of all those involved and, most importantly, the deliverables of the survey itself.

Many perfectly good surveys efforts meet with a less than positive reception because they are not what the client wanted or thought they would be getting. Setting clear goals from the start helps eliminate confusion and lack of clarity during the survey process itself and also helps prevent frustration caused by unmet expectations. Therefore, making underlying assumptions about survey objectives explicit and gaining consensus on key issues and stated outcomes is necessary for the ultimate success of any survey, large or small. Returning to our travel analogy, if each person on the trip has a different set of directions all of which highlight contradictory routes, how can everyone possibly expect to end up at the same destination at the same time? The best route needs to be mapped out in a participative fashion for all to see.

OBTAINING COMMITMENT

In the discussions above we have alluded to the importance of having a stated set of objectives for the survey effort itself. The support, participation and commitment from organizational members is equally important. A well designed and integrated survey will undoubtedly result in wasted effort and frustration on the part of its sponsors if neither senior leadership nor the rank and file acknowledge or understand its use. This is why determining which constituents should be involved in the initial goal-setting and design stages are very important and why we already have placed so much emphasis on it. Clearly, one of the easiest ways to build support and commitment among management and employees is to include them in the survey process from the start.

Let us start with senior management. It can be a relatively easy task to involve them strategically when there is a senior leader willing to sponsor or at least serve as a figurehead for the survey effort (as in our example), but it can be much more difficult when the process has been initiated solely from lower levels in the organization. Some organizations have relatively autonomous line operations capable of supporting a survey effort of their own; however, others can be in the difficult position of having to 'sell' their idea to (i.e., get permission from) their corporate superiors. If a human resources or organization development function is the initiator of a survey effort, there is the likelihood of a negative connotation or attitude backlash on the part of senior management. This backlash often occurs because the senior managers realize that for a not insignificant amount of money and resources they are likely to be:

- seen as targets for all the collective woes of the organization since they are responsible for most policy and strategic decisions, and/or
- expected to actually do something about the results, even if they are extremely negative and/or not within their control.

It is for these reasons that many organization-wide survey efforts are tied to large-scale development and change initiatives (e.g., Kraut, 1996a). There is often an expectation generated among respondents taking the time to complete the survey questionnaire that something will indeed be done, which can be a very real and palpable force to be reckoned with. Senior managers are, indeed, often the target of employees' frustrations, particularly where issues of job security and salary levels are prominent concerns. In our experience, the most successful change-related survey efforts are those that have been used in conjunction with a new or emerging leader, or the introduction of a set of core values or behaviours that are fully supported by the senior ranks.

Survey feedback, for example, was used very effectively after the SmithKline Beecham merger (Burke and Jackson, 1991) as a means to help monitor how

27

much progress the company was making towards achieving its new senior management inspired mission of creating a 'Simply Better' culture. The results of the second survey, about two years later, showed significant improvements in areas such as rewarding and celebrating achievements, utilizing people's skills and abilities, and being more customer-driven rather than profit-driven (Bauman, Jackson and Lawrence, 1997).

Support from senior leadership can provide both the tangible and intangible benefits (e.g., credibility, perceived importance, financial support, decision-making latitude) for reaching the objectives of the survey process. The degree to which senior management support is needed depends to some extent on the purpose of the survey itself – e.g., a general assessment of work space conditions, for example, may require less active participation – but even the simplest of survey projects can benefit from having the stamp of approval from the top of the hierarchy. When the survey effort is part of a more significant change initiative, however, obtaining this support is imperative.

Besides senior management, the other group of people that need to be actively involved in and committed to the survey process are, of course, those at the other end of the hierarchy – i.e., the employees. For the moment we use the term in its broadest sense to encompass all types of organizational members, including middle management ranks. Employees are the backbone of any organization: they represent and enact the social structure and organizational culture on a day-to-day basis. It is for this reason that nothing truly meaningful, whether accurate assessment or fundamental organizational change, can be accomplished without their participation in some manner, even if it is only to clear their desks and physically leave the plant when it is downsized.

Survey efforts are subject to these same social forces as well. They involve asking a large number of people a great many questions about personal perceptions, management behaviours, work conditions and/or the organization in general. When you are planning to conduct an organizational survey, remember that you are fundamentally making two assumptions about the people you intend to assess:

- that they will respond to your questionnaire
- that their responses will be accurate and valid (i.e., reflect their perceptions of the current organizational reality rather than some other set of agenda or anticipated response set).

As we will discuss in Steps 2 to 5, neither of these assumptions should be taken for granted. One way of increasing the validity and utility of the process at the very start of the process, however, is by involving employees at all levels from the beginning. As we mentioned earlier, one of the best mechanisms for ensuring this type of participation is a task force or set of task forces designed to shepherd various aspects of the survey process. These groups of employees can provide an opportunity for obtaining cross-functional and cross-level representation among different organizational constituents. These groups may need the assistance of a trained facilitator to help them work collaboratively rather than competitively, particularly if the differences in perspective among functions or locations is strong, but the end result can be a much more informed, accurate and influential survey process that can truly affect the organization and how it functions.

Of course, the extent to which such task forces can be used varies considerably. In some companies, for example, we have seen the task force approach take the form of a group devoted to a specific issue, such as enhancing team spirit or improving managerial leadership. These more active groups often allow the team to develop a real sense of ownership of their project. They tend to be involved in all aspects of the process, ranging from the identification of key issues and survey objectives, through designing individual items and questionnaire formats, to the recommendation and even implementation of very specific development and improvement initiatives subsequent to the data feedback process.

On the other hand, we have seen some companies use the task force approach as a form of employee representation. In situations like these, the group may be a specific 'survey team' responsible primarily for asserting the 'voice' of the employee on general issues and concerns regarding the process. Sometimes these groups are also used to test the individual items for wording choice or applicability to the workforce across various levels and departments. The idea here is that while these individuals do not really help design the overall objectives or content of the survey, they are involved just enough to promote goodwill and a sense of honesty regarding the effort which, in turn, is intended to communicate a degree of openness and candour to the rest of the organization. Of course, the former, more involved approach to using a task force tends to be more successful than the latter, although they both have their benefits depending on the situation. Either way, however, employees must be involved at least at some level in the survey process or they will not respond.

OVERCOMING RESISTANCE AND APATHY

Another means of involving employees in the survey process at the beginning, and one that tends to be successful at targeting and working through resistance, is the use of focus groups. Focus groups, wherein one or more facilitators have an open discussion with a small group of employees from either similar or divergent areas, can be an invaluable tool not only for data collection and building

29

item content but also as a means of communication and breaking down barriers. When undertaken well, focus groups can be one of the most effective ways of generating positive perceptions of the survey process and converting sceptical or cynical factions into allies. The basic idea here is to provide an objective and safe forum where people can feel comfortable expressing their thoughts, opinions, fears and ideas regarding whatever issues are relevant. We have used focus groups in the past, for example, to explore topics such as positive and negative experiences with prior organizational surveys (regardless of where employees had their exposure), various change initiatives that worked and those that failed, what it takes to be a high performer or to work well in a team in their organization, what types of issues they would like to hear about regarding a survey effort, etc. Even when the issues identified are no longer particularly novel, focus groups remain an excellent mechanism for building trust and support for a survey effort before it gets off the ground. Further, they provide an opportunity to communicate to employees the objectives, importance and level of commitment of the survey, which in some instances can be very important for the success of the effort. Table 1.2 provides a sample protocol that was used in a series of focus groups designed to explore prior survey experiences and future expectations.

One simple decision that has significant implications for creating positive or negative energy in a survey effort, and that must be made at the very start of a survey effort, concerns the confidentiality of the responses obtained. Determining who will have access to the data is of vital concern. If the confidentiality of participants' responses is breached or even suspect in any way, the entire survey process will lose not only its credibility but also its validity. In short, the quickest way to ensure low return rates and 'faked' data is to fail to provide this level of protection. If participants do not feel 100 per cent confident that their individual

Table 1.2   Sample focus group questions for a survey

Please take 10–15 minutes and jot down on a piece of paper your answers to the following questions. Then we will spend an hour or so in the group discussing your issues and concerns.

1. Describe your survey nightmares – what bad results could come from the survey and why?

2. Describe your positive survey expectations and/or experiences.

3. What can we do to make the survey meaningful?

4. What are the main issues facing your organization that you would like to see included on the survey?

5. What are the positives in your organization?

6. If you could make up a 'wish list' for the organization, what would be on it?

assessments and opinions will be kept confidential – i.e., separate from their name or other information capable of identifying them individually – they will either refuse to answer the survey or answer it untruthfully. This is not news to many, but it is surprising how often situations arise that call into question the confidentiality of responses.

For example, on a recent survey project we contracted at the start with our client and with employees throughout the organization, through a series of meetings and focus groups, that we would not process unit or department level reports for groups of employees with fewer than ten members responding. We had all agreed that groupings of this size for this particular organization would guarantee the confidentiality and therefore anonymity of the individual responses. When the time came to actually generate the reports, however, our client was under considerable pressure from his superiors to produce reports for groups of fewer than ten individuals and subsequently was applying a similar level of pressure on us to respond. Despite a clear contracting process with this same individual at the beginning of the survey process, and amid a series of public announcements and discussions with employees of a set policy regarding the confidentiality of the data, there was a strong push to abrogate our pre-existing agreement. After much discussion we were finally able to convince the client to adhere to the original agreement because it was the right thing to do. However, it was a difficult struggle. To be fair, the impetus for our client's request to examine the data at a lower level than originally agreed was to provide small group leaders with specific actionable information, not to point fingers or to be used for staff reduction decisions as can often be the case (and which employees fear the most). Nevertheless, releasing this information would have violated our agreement with employees, damaged the perception of senior management, and served to invalidate any future survey efforts in the organization and probably most other types of organization development initiatives as well.

We hope this example highlights the importance of maintaining ethical practices and policies in the conduct of organizational surveys. Whether one is acting as an internal or external practitioner, educate, advise and inform the client about potential breaches in confidentiality and work with them to do what is best for the organization as well as the individual. We will return to this issue again in later steps.

DECIDING WHAT INFORMATION TO COLLECT

How do you decide what belongs on a survey? What questions should be asked? What types of background or demographic questions should be included? Who should respond to the survey? As one might expect, the answers to all of these

31

questions can be derived from the core objectives and anticipated outcomes of the survey process. Hence we have another reason for making sure that these elements are clearly and firmly established at the beginning of the survey development process. They will not provide a complete blueprint of what content should be included in the instrumentation; however, being clear about these issues does provide a solid guide to follow. The content design is augmented, as we have already noted, through the use of directed focus groups as well as research conducted on archival data (e.g., past surveys, annual reports, newspaper articles, political issues of the past, consulting reports, etc.). In some organizations, a conceptual model or framework (e.g., Burke and Litwin, 1992; Nadler and Tushman, 1992; Weisbord, 1978) is also used to help provide a more broadly based picture of the organization – particularly when the survey is intended to be more diagnostic in nature. In others, there may be a simple series of questions or issues that someone has in mind with firm plans for assessment. Of course, the danger with this latter approach, although common enough, is that without having conducted some degree of research or discussion on the nature of the issue being studied or incorporating some broader organizational model or framework capable of identifying unanticipated relationships, the survey effort runs the risk of being stilted and limited in its interpretive abilities. Once again, the extent to which this is a problem for the survey practitioner depends in large part on the objectives and scope of the survey effort. Still, it is always better to have more information rather than less when designing the specific contents. Since it is often the case that the survey effort itself is often intended to help define the parameters of the issues in the organization, the use of an existing organizational model capable of providing detailed analysis is highly recommended.

Step 2 will discuss primarily the specifics of designing survey items and formats, so it is appropriate here to speak briefly about the inclusion of other types of information. Because a successful survey effort is one that has a significant amount of forethought involved, it follows that the inclusion of various demographic and/or background variables is critical to allowing the data to be used in the manner in which it was intended. For example, in the financial services organization mentioned earlier, where the head of the diversity council was intent on using the survey to examine employee perceptions by various subgroups, it would have been extremely damaging to the survey effort if we had not ultimately included questions on respondent gender, age and ethnicity, among others. There is always a balance being struck (see Figure 1.3) between asking too many of these types of identifying items (since they could indeed conceivably be used to single out individual responses) and not including enough of the items necessary to complete the survey objectives.

In some surveys, for example in those organizations where employee trust in

32

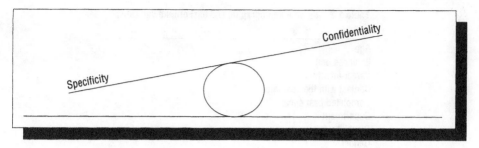

Figure 1.3 **Balancing assessment priorities**

the organizational and/or in the confidentiality of the assessment process is low, this might mean rejecting some items that might provide for interesting analyses and keep only those that are absolutely necessary. In discussions with the members of the survey team in a financial services organization, it was decided that while gender, ethnicity, age and education would be retained for analysis purposes (bearing in mind the ten person per group response protection mentioned earlier) marital status, child responsibility and religious affiliation were ruled out as being both too intrusive and too specific in conjunction with the other questions. However, any number of possible items of this nature can be included as long as the appropriate balance has been struck. Table 1.3 provides a partial list of many of these types of variables. Many of these items may seem overly intrusive to some people, and some would certainly be considered illegal to ask of potential job applicants under formal hiring procedures, but a survey is always voluntary in nature (at its very core) and therefore respondents always have the choice to either leave the item blank, provide a false response, or not respond to the survey at all.

At this point, with firm objectives, anticipated outcomes, and the appropriate level of involvement from key constituents in the organization, you are now ready to proceed to the next stage of the survey process – i.e., the development of the content itself.

CHECKLIST FOR STEP 1

1. Set clear strategic objectives regarding the purpose and uses of the survey.
   • Determine the purpose and objectives of the survey before you begin – why the survey is being conducted and what will be achieved.
   • Draw a road-map, or a guide to show you how to get where you want to go.

Table 1.3   Sample demographic and background variables

Age
Business unit
Career intentions
Contact with the customer
Completed past survey
Department
Disability
Gender
Grade
Education
Employer prior to merger or acquisition
Employment status
Ethnic affiliation
Functional group
Job type
Length of service with the organization
Length of service in current job
Location of primary work site
Management level
Nationality
Number of people supervised
Payroll category
Regional location
Religious affiliation
Supervisory status
Training exposure
Years of experience in a managerial or supervisory position
Years of experience with your present manager
Work schedule

- Identify a marker at the end that tells you when you have reached your goals.

2. Obtain commitment from senior management and employees.
   - Gain the support, participation and commitment from organizational members.
   - Determine which constituents should be involved in goal-setting and design stages:
     - start with senior management
     - involve human resources or organization development functions
     - involve high potentials and well-respected employees
     - set up task forces.

3. Identify and overcome negative energy and apathy.
   - Gather information about survey perceptions:
     - conduct focus groups to identify problem areas
     - speak with employees about past survey experiences.
   - Communicate plans to deal with issues before surveying.

4. Decide what types of information should be collected.
   - Include content areas such as leadership perceptions, culture, performance.
   - Identify background information such as age, gender, tenure, etc.

Developing a world-class survey

Ask a stupid question, get a stupid answer.

Unknown

This step deals with the second stage in the survey process – i.e., developing the content (the specific questions) of the survey instrumentation itself. Like good contracting, good item development and construction can have a profound and long-lasting impact on the success or failure of any survey effort. All the fancy statistical modelling in the world and dazzling presentation skills replete with bells and whistles and smoke and mirrors cannot mask an obviously flawed survey instrument. If the design is poor, the results and their interpretation are likely to be as well. Therefore, mastering the art and science of good, solid, logical survey construction is of paramount importance to any practitioner venturing forth in this arena.

This step concentrates on the elements involved in the design and development of a world-class survey tool. Through examples and descriptions of prior research and experience, the survey practitioner is guided on the importance of using teamwork to build quality surveys; gathering, identifying and working through key issues that need to be assessed; drafting a survey instrument; and testing and refining it for final administration. By the end of this section, practitioners should have a better understanding of how to write items that are (a) specific, (b) clear and concise, (c) free of jargon and other biases, (d) based on sound psychometric theory and research, and (e) appropriate for the respondents to whom they are going to be administered.

In addition to the issue of survey design and item writing which is the main subject of this section, there is a fundamental question regarding instrumentation that must first be addressed in any survey effort – does the survey team want to use a standardized and/or existing tool or create a customized one of their own? We are assuming here that the survey team has chosen to create their own customized tool; however, this is not the only option in the survey process. In fact, many organizations do choose to use an existing instrument that has standardized, highly tested, well-used items that also have useful and relevant norms collected from other organizations and/or groups. A custom-designed survey tool can include some questions, unmodified of course, that have been used in other settings for similar comparative analyses but, by its very nature, a freshly designed survey instrument cannot match a standardized product taken 'off the shelf' with respect to the quality or quantity of external normative comparisons. Conversely, standardized tools because of their applicability to a wide range of settings, are often unlikely to be able to capture in enough depth and/or assess the specific nature of the information required in many organization survey efforts. Standard surveys questionnaires can be very useful for comparison purposes (also known as external bench-marking), and can be cheaper and faster to implement, but they are not well suited to organizational survey efforts initiated in response to some significant and specific set of objectives such as those resulting from a large-scale change effort or a merger or acquisition situation for example. And, since it is our view that most successful survey efforts do need to have specific goals and objectives to be effective, the utility of a standardized instrument is likely to be questionable in these types of situations. Even if the survey team does decide to choose a standard product for any number of reasons, the information contained in this chapter should be useful in evaluating the design quality of the products that are being reviewed for possible use.

USING A SURVEY DESIGN TEAM

Developing a survey that is (a) successful in capturing or measuring what it is supposed to, (b) well received, and (c) actionable is not a simple task. To construct a survey that meets these criteria it is often wise to convene or assemble a survey design team (Rea and Parker, 1992). In some instances this may be the same group as the survey team or task force mentioned in Step 1 for generating discussion about important issues to be assessed, in other situations this group may be an entirely different set of employees – e.g., comprised in large part of experts or experienced practitioners in the fields of survey item design and construction (see Figure 2.1). Since the purpose of this team is to design the core content of the survey instrument itself, this requires a narrower set of skills than those required for the general project planning and testing phases.

The notion of a survey design team may bring to mind the catch-phrase 'there is safety in numbers', the purpose here is really more appropriately reflected in the axiom 'two heads are better than one'. This group is not intended to serve as a means for diffusing responsibility. Instead, the design team's basic function is to create clear, easy to understand items for inclusion in the assessment instru-

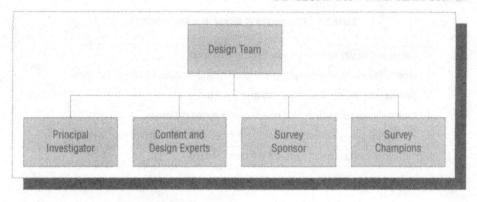

Figure 2.1 The survey design team

ment. This team is assembled by the principal survey investigator or sponsor for the sole purpose of item development. The survey design team should consist not only of technical and content experts, but also of key players in the organiza- tion – i.e., high potential employees, current and future opinion leaders, etc. As emphasized in our discussion of the objective-setting process in Step 1, involve a few strategically placed, highly visible and credible members of management and/or senior leadership to help establish the importance of the survey initiative. However, since the design team is clearly more task oriented than the basic plan- ning group referred to earlier, it is often difficult to obtain any significant level of participation from senior level individuals at this tactical a level. There often needs to be a degree of balance between involving senior individuals involved in the planning and goal-setting phase, and having their input in the item construc- tion phase. This may, of course, be somewhat less of an issue in those organiza- tions where the CEO or the senior management board is the key driving force behind the survey effort.

In any case, once a survey design team has been assembled and briefed as to the specific nature of the survey (e.g., contractual arrangements regarding roles and deliverables, the survey purpose and objectives, the timeline for the roll-out process, the key players and supporters involved, the cost constraints, etc.), item development can begin. The item development process should follow the series of five steps outlined in Table 2.1. Each of these is described in greater detail below.

Table 2.1   Five phases of survey item development

1. **Gather** preliminary information about important issues.

2. **Identify** key issues by summarizing and integrating all available sources of information.

3. **Discuss** your findings with those who gave you input.

4. **Draft** the initial survey document based on your agreed key issues.

5. **Pre-test** the survey with your representative group and other organizational members.

Source: Adapted and expanded from Rea and Parker, 1992

GATHERING PRELIMINARY INFORMATION

Many clients as well as practitioners often have very clear ideas about the types of issues and questions that they would like to see included in a given survey effort; however, it is always best to gather information from a variety of sources prior to the initiation of any significant survey item development work. As discussed in Step 1, conducting focus groups with a cross-section of employees is often an excellent source for generating a list of issues, problems and concerns that could be woven into a survey assessment tool. Other tools than can be quite effective include individual interviews with various members of senior management and/or functional heads, mini-surveys or questionnaires with write-in questions distributed to a small select group of individuals, corporate communications and documents, articles written about the organization in the external media, as well as other types of archival data such as prior surveys, consulting reports or planning projects previously completed. These latter sources of information can be useful in identifying consistent patterns or trends in the organization's development, but the most useful data is that which has been gathered in an open forum where issues, questions and ideas can be discussed and debated. This is why focus groups are the most commonly used and appreciated technique for collecting this type of preliminary information for the purposes of survey development. Focus groups provide members of the survey design team with the opportunity to discuss in depth and probe possible survey items and issues with a representative sample of participants. Issues inherent in the process itself, such as concerns regarding confidentiality or the purpose and importance of the survey effort, can also be raised and therefore better dealt with in the communication and administration phases.

IDENTIFYING KEY ISSUES

Once you have conducted your preliminary data-gathering sessions (e.g., through focus groups, interviews etc.), it is time to begin the data synthesis process. You will probably begin to see initial patterns emerge in your preliminary data after your third or fourth data-gathering session. Unless you already have a standard framework or guide for organizing the information obtained such as the Burke–Litwin model (Burke and Litwin, 1992) or Nadler and Tushman's (1992) congruence model, these early patterns can be used to provide you with potential categories of issues or main themes for classifying and quantifying the data. Frameworks, whether pre-existing or created on the spot, are important because they provide us with a way to view the world in an organized fashion. Through the use of such models it is also possible to identify linkages between issues and concepts, which in turn can be used for future initiatives and action planning (more on this in Steps 5 and 6). You will need to have a clear and concise method for categorizing all the comments and perceptions you have collected in this initial step of the development process.

For many consultants and survey practitioners the use of a simple 2×2 model is often an important diagnostic tool for working with such data. In this way, members of a survey team can present and/or work with complex data directly and easily. Figure 2.2 shows a sample of how data can be organized and presented using this simple dichotomous approach. In this example, let us assume that company XYZ is interested in undertaking a large-scale organizational survey of all employees to determine areas for change within the organization. Focus groups and interviews are then conducted with a cross-section of the organizational membership to identify the areas most in need of change and to assess the perceived difficulty in achieving this change. The 2×2 model in Figure 2.2 provides a simple comparative framework for looking at all the issues raised during the data-gathering effort. Based on the results displayed in this model, items in the full employee survey would be best directed at the topics described in the 'Long-Term Goals' and 'Quick Gains' sections since these areas represent content that is of high priority but can also be changed (either in the short or long term). The nature of the messages to be communicated to employees about the expected speed of action that will be taken as a result of the survey effort, may temper the extent to which items reflecting quick gains are emphasized over those based on the more long-term goals. On the other hand, items reflecting the 'Low Priority' and 'Easy to Change' section, while useful to include from the standpoint of having issues that can be actioned quickly, are not likely to have much impact since their importance is relatively low. Similarly, the issues noted in the 'Not Likely to Change' section are, for the most part, best ignored in the survey because the assessment of opinions in these areas is only

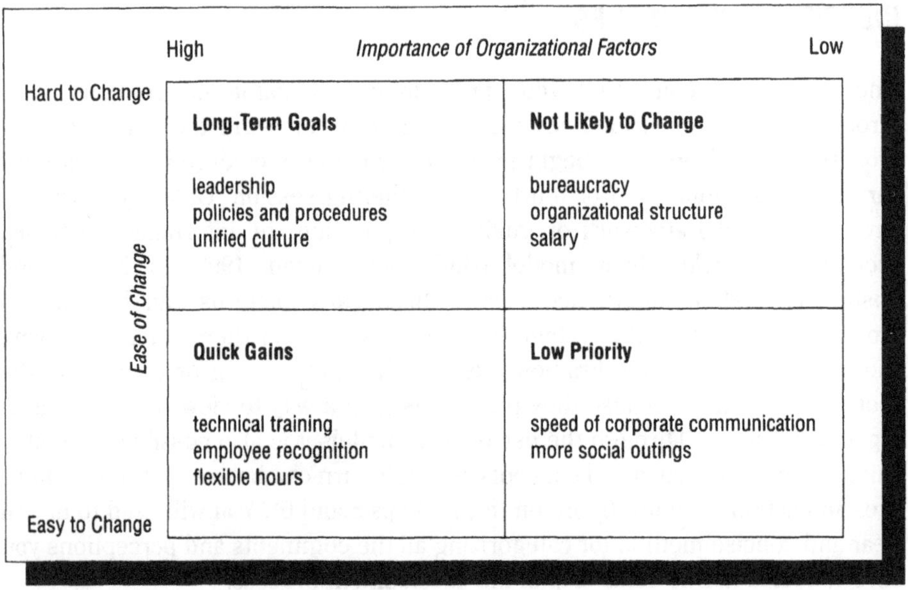

Figure 2.2   Classic 2 × 2 model: summary of interviews and focus groups for company XYZ

likely to raise expectations that will probably not be met for some time, given their relatively low priority and difficult nature. Members of the survey design team need to find some mechanism to identify the key issues that can be changed as well as those that need to be changed in order to build a survey effort that will have significant and meaningful results for people.

DISCUSSING YOUR FINDINGS

When you ask people for their advice, opinions and ideas they want to know that you have understood and appreciated what they have had to say. From the perspective of survey design, this means you need to present the findings of your data-gathering efforts not only to the survey sponsor, but also, at least in a summary form, to those participants who provided you with input from the focus groups and interviews. Often this feedback loop affords an opportunity to verify that the issues you think are important and deserving of item content, based on your synthesis of the results, are the same ones that others want to see reflected in the survey instrument.

A written report that summarizes your key findings is often a good approach

Table 2.2   Sample memo to survey sponsor

To: Mai Client
From: The Principal Investigator of the XYZ Survey Team
RE: Key Issues

Dear Mai,

I hope everything is going well. I am enclosing a brief synthesis of the key issues on which to concentrate in our survey identified by the XYZ Survey Team, based on our recent interviews and focus groups conducted in your organization. Please review these findings to see if they coincide with your assessment of the key issues for your organization. We would like to incorporate these into our draft version of the survey.

If you have any questions or comments regarding our findings, please call.

---

to take. The format of this report can be based on a simple categorical approach, similar to the one described above, that serves to prioritize key issues along a set of dimensions (e.g., high to low importance, positive versus negative change, high to low degree of changeability), or it can be based on a more structured approach along the lines of the classic OD technique of content coding responses (similar to the sample described in Table 2.3). The data collected in this initial gathering step should be presented in a clear manner that highlights the issues the survey design team have found to be the most important. Tables 2.2 and 2.3 show a sample memo and synthesis of some key issues based on a series of employee focus groups that demonstrate a good example of this type of approach.

DRAFTING THE INITIAL SURVEY DOCUMENT

The next step in the survey design sequence is the actual drafting of the pilot survey document. This is easily the most complicated and labour-intensive phase of survey development. Figure 2.3 provides an overview of the basic steps involved in the process. Almost anyone can formulate a simple question to ask, but not everyone can write a valid and reliable survey item. There is much more to developing the contents of a survey questionnaire than simply writing items, many of which will be covered in more detail below.

It is necessary to the success of the survey effort that the design team, in conjunction with the client, sponsor or end user of the survey results, spends time at the outset defining some of the more general parameters of the item writing process before any drafting even begins. Key questions to consider here include:

Table 2.3   Sample synthesis of key issues

Focus Group Questions
1. What are the barriers and hindrances you experience in your work?
2. What is exciting about your work?

Focus Group Participants
Focus groups were with 200 company XYZ employees from all levels, functions and locations within the organization.

Barriers to your work
Poor work-life balance (120 responses)
- I'd like to have more balance between work and personal life.
- I wish I had more time to spend with my family.
- Workload.
- Lack of support for home life.

Lack of team focus (98 responses)
- Bureaucratic process, no team emphasis.
- Not a lot of teamwork and co-ordination.
- Lack of co-ordination between departments.

Exciting about work
I like the people (133 responses)
- Like the people – bright, energetic, creative.
- The people.
- Personal relationships.
- Working with people.

Nature of work (99 responses)
- It's different every day.
- The work we do is important.
- Nature of the projects. I feel very fortunate.

Given freedom and autonomy (22 responses)
- Like running my own programme.
- Like to be managed loosely.

- What is the maximum number of items we want to have in the survey?
- Should the questions all use the same scale or a variety of different ones?
- Are one or two items enough to cover main topic areas or do there need to be more?
- Should the survey be short and densely packed or well spaced and easy to read?

By clarifying and delineating at the start many of these types of parameters for the survey instrument in terms of content and presentation, it will help all parties involved, including the survey design team, achieve greater clarity about the end

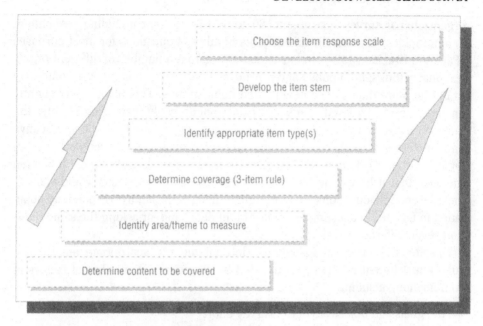

Figure 2.3 The item construction process map

product they are working to achieve. Much like good contracting, defining the look and feel of the survey early on and with significant specificity can save a great deal of heartache and unmet expectations later on in the process. The remainder of this section details the pros and cons of the wide range of options for survey design, layout, item construction and response formats.

SURVEY LENGTH

As a former consulting colleague of ours was often fond of saying, 'size isn't everything'. However, when it comes to survey development, the size or length of the assessment instrument is indeed an important consideration. The objective of the survey design team is to formulate a questionnaire that is (a) long enough to capture all the essential content elements that need to be measured, but (b) not so long as to increase the likelihood that respondents will be intimidated by its size and hence fail to complete it or complete it with reduced accuracy.

The possible range is unlimited. We have seen surveys, for example, ranging from only four or five questions to over 250 items. While there is no 'magic number' when it comes to determining the appropriate length of an organizational survey instrument, 80 to 100 items (not including respondent demographics) is generally an adequate number of questions for most purposes (Paul and Bracken, 1995). In our experience across a number of different organizational settings, both public and private, a survey instrument should contain up to but no more than 150 content-related items in total. This tends to err slightly on the side of increased numbers of data points while increasing slightly the burden on respondents; however, in practice we have found it to be an effective limit in terms of both the level and quality of data received as well psychologically when working with clients and trying to meet their demands. It is often the case that if he or she had their choice, the survey sponsor would want to include enough questions to thoroughly alienate the entire respondent population in favour of collecting every last bit of detail and/or asking the same question seven different ways.

Despite these general guidelines, determining the appropriate length of a survey instrument is often best decided by considering a number of factors in combination, including:

- the goals and objectives of the survey effort
- the background characteristics of the respondent group
- the budget for the assessment project
- the method of survey administration (see Step 4)
- the type and format of the items of interest
- expected turnaround.

Remember that the goal of the survey construction process is to design a tool that is both concise and comprehensive (Edwards et al., 1997). Table 2.4 provides an overview of some of the potential differences between a 'shorter' survey effort and a substantially 'larger' one for each of the above factors. Any combination of the above factors can be considered when designing a survey instrument, those in Table 2.4 provide some general preferences based solely on survey size.

NUMBER OF ITEMS PER CONTENT AREA

Another issue that needs to be considered when designing a survey instrument is the number of items assigned to measure each content or topic area (e.g., leadership, communication, employee satisfaction). A good and often used rule of thumb with respect to this issue is three to five questions of coverage per concept or theme. The thinking behind this simple formula is that each content area should be asked from several different vantage points to ensure complete coverage. Here is an example. The items presented in Table 2.5 were designed to measure the degree of teamwork experienced by employees in company XYZ.

46

Table 2.4   Potential differences between characteristics in shorter and longer survey efforts

		80 items or more			
Goals	Group membership	Budget	Method	Type of item	Expected turnaround
In-depth survey	Non-managers	Larger	Paper Computer	Close-ended	Ample time

		Less than 80 items			
Goals	Group membership	Budget	Method	Type of item	Expected turnaround
Quick assessment	Managers	Smaller	Interview Voice response	Open-ended	Little time

As you can see, the questions assess the level of teamwork at the organizational, business unit and individual work group levels. By including items that access this concept at each of these levels of organizational analysis, the data collected will provide the survey practitioner with a better understanding of the specific nature of teamwork in company XYZ.

In most surveys, having more than five questions on a specific concept borders on redundancy. Having too many questions on the same topic, unless these represent distinctly different facets of behaviour such as the broader area of managerial behaviour, runs the risk of unnecessarily increasing response

Table 2.5   Sample items to assess teamwork in company XYZ

To what extent does the XYZ culture foster teamwork?

①	②	③	④	⑤	⑥
Culture does not foster teamwork				Culture fosters teamwork	

To what extent is there an integrated culture among the business units in company XYZ (i.e., a unified approach to accomplishing work)?

①	②	③	④	⑤	⑥
Culture is poorly integrated				Culture is highly integrated	

To what extent do work group members co-operate in accomplishing work?

①	②	③	④	⑤	⑥
Work group members work individually – not much interaction or co-operation				Work group members rely on each other and collaborate to get the job done	

47

Table 2.6 Sample overlapping items

1. To what extent are employees motivated in company XYZ?
2. How motivated do you feel in your job?
3. How motivated are you to do your job well?
4. To what extent do managers motivate employees?

burden as well as potentially irritating respondents. Even if the items are well dispersed throughout the survey instrument, respondents are likely to identify those that appear to assess the same construct. They often point this out to survey practitioners even when, as in some cases, the items are intended to assess more subtle differences in perspective. Table 2.6 provides an example of four different items, which when originally designed, were intended to measure different facets of motivation but probably represent too much overlap in content.

Of course, the questions in Table 2.6 may be too similar in focus but it is possible that employees will rate these items somewhat differently – a hypothesis that can actually be tested during the pilot phase of the design process before final administration – and/or that the survey sponsor may want to include all these items, regardless of the level of overlap, for other reasons (e.g., the message communicated in the inclusion of four separate items assessing employee motivation, etc.).

TWO TYPES OF SURVEY ITEMS

Survey items, like people, come in many different shapes and sizes. They can be long (wordy) or short (simple). They can be qualitative or quantitative in nature. They can be designed to assess facts or attitudes. They can be measured on nominal-, ordinal- or interval-level scales. They can ask how you feel or how other employees feel about a given topic. However, there are two very broad basic categories into which all survey items must fit. These two general categories consist of *open-* and *close-ended* questions (Edwards et al., 1997; Fink, 1995). Each of these item types has advantages and disadvantages associated with its use.

Open-ended or write-in questions

Open-ended or write-in questions ask survey respondents to provide an answer to a given question in their own words. These types of questions do not have a limited range of responses since their boundaries are defined solely by the respondents themselves, and are also very similar to essay questions found in many school examinations. Here are some examples of typical open-ended survey items reflecting different types of content:

1. How long have you been at company XYZ?
2. How clear are employees about the mission of company XYZ?
3. To what extent does company XYZ value its employees?

Question 1 is designed to elicit a simple numerical response; questions 2 and 3 are more general in nature and could result in a variety of responses. There are several significant benefits of open-ended questions:

1. They are less sterile and/or flat than close-ended questions – i.e., they can enrich and enlighten one's understanding of the data collected by adding a more descriptive human element.
2. People can answer these types of questions from their own unique perspective instead of being forced into the response options that are driven by the paradigm of the survey practitioner or design team. In this way they allow for a greater degree of individuality and expansiveness on the part of the respondent.
3. They allow people the often much needed opportunity to let off steam. Open-ended items do provide an effective avenue for catharsis.
4. Lastly, and perhaps most importantly, as stated above these types of questions allow respondents to answer in their own words (Edwards et al., 1997).

Because of the complexity of analysing and standardizing responses obtained from open-ended questions, it is generally considered good industry practice to use them sparingly and in conjunction with a number of close-ended items. In fact, some practitioners recommend that organizational surveys contain easy-to-read, close-ended items wherever possible (Rea and Parker, 1992). We think this recommendation may be a bit too strong. In our view, a well conceived and constructed survey instrument should include a balanced complement of both these basic item types.

While open-ended questions can and do provide the survey practitioner with rich data, which can lead to a better, more in-depth understanding of respondents' issues and concerns, they do have several serious limitations that should be recognized and factored in when constructing and implementing an organizational survey tool. The main disadvantages of the open-ended format include:

1. The time required on the part of respondents for completion is considerably longer.
2. They are much more time-consuming for the practitioner and/or survey task force to content code and analyse.

Table 2.7   Sample close-ended questions

---

1. How long have you been at company XYZ?
   01   Less than 1 year
   02   1–5 years
   03   6–10 years
   04   11–15 years
   05   16 years or more

2. How clear are employees about the mission of company XYZ?

   ①   ②   ③   ④   ⑤   ⑩
   Not clear   Moderately   Very clear
                            clear

3. To what extent does company XYZ value its employees?

   ①   ②   ③   ④   ⑤   ⑩
   To no   To a moderate   To a very
   extent   extent   great extent

---

3. By their very unstructured nature they have a tendency to produce redundant and/or extraneous information.
4. They rarely assess the level of intensity of a given issue, feeling or concern.

Close-ended questions

The other basic type of survey question is the close-ended question. Close-ended items, the most popular of formats, by design present a question and a limited number of options from which respondents must make one or more choices. Examples of these can be found on any True/False or multiple choice test. Table 2.7 lists examples of close-ended survey items. It should be apparent to the reader that while these same questions were asked in the open-ended example above, the quality and quantity of information that can be obtained from the close-ended format is very different. While responses to question 1 would probably be very similar, questions 2 and 3 in this format would produce a very different type of information than might be collected when used in a write-in method.

There are a number of benefits of close-ended questions that make them particularly useful for survey practitioners:

1. They are fast and easy for the respondent to answer.
2. They provide data that are easy to understand and interpret.
3. They ensure uniform responses across respondents in different functions, areas and even organizations, thus making comparisons simple and efficient.
4. They provide the respondent with helpful memory cues to facilitate some sort of response.

5. They can remind respondents of ideas or potential options that were unknown or forgotten (Edwards et al., 1997; Rea and Parker, 1992).

Of course, the close-ended format has its disadvantages as well. For example:

1. The questions chosen to be included in the survey instrument may not be representative of people's attitudes and opinions regarding a certain content area.
2. These types of items compel respondents to express attitudes even if they truly do not have them.
3. The response options provided may not reflect the full range of needs or opinions.

Despite these problems, however, close-ended items are extremely popular in organizational assessment survey efforts.

Types of close-ended questions: measurement scales

There are three different levels of measurement available to the survey practitioner when working with close-ended items: categorical/nominal, ordinal and interval (Fink, 1995; Rea and Parker, 1992). Each of these levels provides a different type of data, and each is useful to the survey design team in grouping specific sets of items or variables in a particular way. The various properties of these levels are described below in order of increasing complexity.

Categorical/nominal variables Categorical or nominal variables – representing the most basic type of close-ended questions – are comprised of those items such as gender, ethnicity, religion, political party membership, prior exposure to a survey effort, etc., that can be broken down into discretely different *categories* or groups in order to determine the relative frequency of each response. These categories are often arbitrarily labelled by the survey practitioner in a numerical fashion. However, since the data collected from these types of items do not inherently possess differences in magnitude or size, the assigned numerical values on a questionnaire, for example, would be for identification purposes only. There is no implied difference in valuation. By attaching numerical values to these types of variables, however, survey practitioners are able to take non-numerical concepts and measure them quantitatively in the form of the frequency of responses selected. As you can see in the following example, the numerical system assigned to gender is for descriptive purposes only.

Example:
What is your gender?
1. Female
2. Male

51

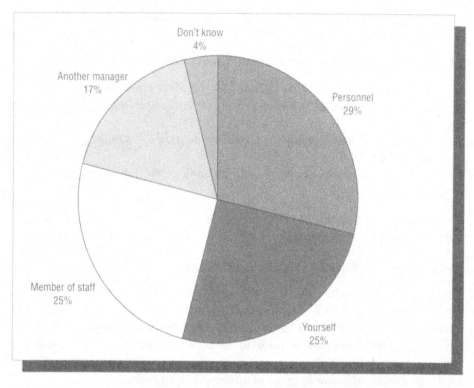

Figure 2.4 Responses to categorical survey question regarding employees' understanding of other individuals or groups that hold a record of their performance appraisal*
Note: *Percentages are based on total number of choices selected and are not forced to be mutually exclusive.

While gender is a relatively simple example, a more complex version of this type of item, yet one that provides important information none the less, is displayed in Figure 2.4.

The only real limitation with nominal-level items, although it is indeed a signif-icant one, is that because the data collected do not really reflect a numerical rela-tionship, the data are somewhat more limited with respect to the types of statistical techniques and analyses that can be used.

Ordinal variables Ordinal-level variables are those variables that have response options that differ in magnitude or size, but are not exactly and propor-tionally different from each other. In effect, these variables are used for ranking different *ranges or groupings*. Some of the most common examples of ordinal-level items found on organizational surveys are such factors as educational level, supervisory status and grade level. In fact, survey instruments tend to have more ordinal measures than any other type (Fink, 1995).

A scale that measures the extent to which a condition is present or absent, for example, is an ordinal-level item. This type of item is used when there are clear differences expected in the relative magnitude of the construct being measured on the survey, but it is not possible to specify if these differences are absolute. Let us consider the construct of empowerment.

Example:
To what extent are you empowered to do your job as you see fit?

①   ②   ③   ④   ⑤   (DK)

To no extent   To a moderate extent   To a very great extent

Most people would agree that there are likely to be differences in the extent to which employees feel empowered to do their jobs effectively. Most would also agree that these differences in perceptions of the level of empowerment experienced simply cannot be measured as accurately as individual differences in height, weight or age. Even in organizations with highly rigid and autocratic cultures, it is highly unlikely that there is absolutely no level of empowerment experienced; it is probably just very limited or infrequent. For these very reasons ordinal-level items are often used for measuring social psychological constructs or phenomena because they allow the survey practitioner a greater degree of specificity than nominal categorical scales but do not make the mistake of assuming precise or absolute differences.

Interval/numerical variables The final type of close-ended question that can be developed for a survey instrument is the interval or numeric item. An interval-level variable provides the survey practitioner with the most precise type of measure available to an organizational survey. Questions designed according to these standards are used when a precise difference can be assessed among discrete scale points or anchors. Some of the most frequently used examples of interval scales are age, tenure, income, height, weight, IQ, temperature, etc., simply because the range of options can be designed to be equidistant from one another (e.g., in five-year blocks).

Example:
Length of service in company XYZ:
a. 1 to 5 years
b. 6 to 10 years
c. 11 to 15 years
d. 16 to 20 years

e. 21 to 25 years

f. 26 to 30 years

Types of close-ended scales: summary

As discussed above, ordinal-level items are the most frequently used of the three close-ended measurement scale types in organizational survey instruments. The popularity of these types of scales derives largely from the latitude they provide survey practitioners in developing items. They are also favoured because of the limitless possibilities they provide in terms of response scale options. There are a great many options for these types of items. Table 2.8 provides an overview of just a few of the more commonly used response categories on organizational surveys instruments.

HOW MANY RESPONSE OPTIONS?

Each of the scales detailed in Table 2.8 consist of five points, anchors or response options, but survey scales of this type can range from as few as two points to as many as will continue to provide a meaningful degree of discrimina-

Table 2.8 Types of response options

	1	2	3	4	5
Endorsement	definitely false	false	don't know	true	definitely true
Frequency	never	almost never	sometimes	very often	always
Intensity	none	very mild	mild	moderate	severe
Influence	no problem	very small problem	small problem	moderate problem	big problem
Comparison	much less than others	somewhat less than others	about the same as others	somewhat more than others	much more than others
Satisfaction	very dissatisfied	dissatisfied	neutral	satisfied	very satisfied
Effectiveness	very ineffective	ineffective	neutral	effective	very effective
Quality	very poor	poor	average	good	very good
Expectancy	much worse than expected	worse than expected	as expected	better than expected	much better than expected
Extent	to no extent	to a small extent	to a moderate extent	to a great extent	to a very great extent
Agreement	strongly disagree	disagree	neutral	agree	strongly agree

Source: (Edwards, et al., 1997; Fink, 1995)

tion. Some questions might warrant a simple set of options such as agree, disagree or neutral, others such as the empowerment example provided above are best measured using a more graduate set of options ranging in magnitude. In practice, organization assessment surveys items usually provide five-, seven- or nine-point options (Fink, 1995), particularly when they have been designed to assess slightly more intangible organizational, behavioural and/or social psychological content areas (e.g., the quality of senior leadership, the degree of responsiveness to the external environment, the usefulness of corporate information mechanisms) – i.e., the primary concern of most survey efforts. Scales can consist of even-numbered anchors (e.g., four, six, eight points) as well, but these types of items are less common in practice because they do not allow for the possibility of a neutral midpoint, particularly in items with scales that are bipolar in nature (described in more detail in the next section).

Some survey practitioners prefer to use these types of even scales to artificially force respondents to make a positive or negative selection (in items with bipolar scales) or at least in the direction of more or less (in those items with a single unipolar extent or magnitude scale) because they feel that it provides more poignant data. However, this process actually adds a level of response bias to the process that cannot be removed in subsequent examination and analyses, which could in turn lead to more spurious findings and recommendations. It is always possible, for example, to explore what would happen to the data if the respondents who chose the midpoint were simply removed on an item-by-item basis during the analysis phase. The practitioner should try to remember that although too much information can always be reduced, it can never be expanded. This is one reason why an early initial meeting with the survey design team and the survey sponsor to define the working parameters and expectations of the survey instrument is an important first step in the design process.

UNIPOLAR VERSUS BIPOLAR RESPONSE OPTIONS

Besides the total number of response options offered, another issue in survey item construction concerns whether or not the questions will be rated using a scale that is unipolar or bipolar in nature. Unipolar response scales are those in which the response can range solely in the relative degree of magnitude of the given statement or phenomena. Examples of these include extent scales (e.g., 'the extent to which employees feel empowered in their jobs') as well as frequency scales. Any item that ranges from nothing to something represents a type of unipolar assessment. Conversely, a bipolar response scaled item provides the survey respondent with two different options that can vary in meaning, on either end of the scale. Agree–disagree scales are a good example of this type of scale. Neither option is necessarily better than the other, but remember that unipolar scales provide the respondent with a greater range of subtlety in terms of response options, while a bipolar scale limits the degree of options by adding a more specific level of detail to the data collected. Two sample scales are provided in the following example that highlight some of the differences between these response options.

Example:
Question – My business unit has clear-cut goals

Unipolar scale	*Bipolar scale*
1 To no extent	1 Strongly disagree
2 To a little extent	2 Disagree
3 To some extent	3 Neither agree nor disagree/neutral
4 To a great extent	4 Agree
5 To a very great extent	5 Strongly agree

If the respondent were to agree with this statement, there are four levels of extent available on the unipolar scale but only two options on the bipolar scale. On the other hand, if the respondent were to disagree with the statement made, there is only one option on the extent scale and that does not even directly assess the level of disagreement, while there are two clear choices on the bipolar scale that would more accurately reflect his or her opinion on this issue. In the end, the best choice regarding these response scale types is made based on the nature of the content being assessed (e.g., does the survey team care about relative presence of the phenomena in the workplace or whether or not the idea elicits a positive or negative opinion) in the survey instrument and the ease and relevance with which these different approaches fit the questions being asked.

GUIDELINES FOR SURVEY CONSTRUCTION

Having obtained a solid understanding of the differences among the various types of items and response scales that can be used, it is now time to turn to some basic rules of thumb with respect to survey item construction. These generally agreed-on principles apply to all types of items and to all survey efforts. Practitioners and their survey design teams should keep these in mind when developing their instruments (Edwards et al., 1997; Fink, 1995; Jones and Bearley, 1995). A brief synopsis of these principles is presented here.

Keep the issues in mind

One of the pitfalls or unexpected negative side-effects of using a survey development team is the tendency for people to become fixated on their own beliefs or values about the necessity of certain survey items that, in reality, may or may not be appropriate to the assessment effort. Team members often have such a vested interest in pursuing issues that they personally believe to be important that even when confronted with the question of relevancy, they continue to promote their item agenda. If taken too far, a survey instrument can quickly become overly long, unwieldy and off target due to such pressures. While this outcome may not have been the intention of the members of the survey design team when advocating for their issue, it can easily be the end result. To a large extent having a conceptual framework such as the Burke–Litwin model (Burke and Litwin, 1992) surrounding the design and analysis process and/or a thorough examination of the preliminary data gathered can help the survey practitioner reduce this risk.

Another force that can affect the aim of the group is the intragroup process itself (Schein, 1988). Sometimes, a bad group process can quickly undermine even the best strategy or integrated organization development framework, resulting in a survey instrument that has been designed by a committee rather than by a team. Therefore, when the team is engaged in developing survey items it is often a good idea to have one of the members take responsibility for monitoring the group process and progress – i.e., to serve as a process consultant (Schein 1988) – to help the team stay on course. This means keeping track of what the key issues are for the organization and goals of the survey effort, and making sure that individual members of the development team do not deviate too far from these objectives in pursuit of their own personal agenda.

In the end, what you ask is what you get. The practitioner must never forget that once the heat of the moment has passed and the data have been collected, there is no turning back to fix a bad item or add one last item that was dropped in favour of something else. Remembering the needs and wants of the survey sponsor and keeping these in mind should be foremost in the thoughts of the survey design team.

Be parsimonious

This principle is related to the comments made earlier regarding the appropriate number of items needed to measure a given construct or issue. Use enough items to measure what you need on a given topic, but not to excess. As previously mentioned, one rule of thumb for the total length of the survey instrument is somewhere between 80 and 100 items (Paul and Bracken, 1995). Many topics may be of interest, but if they are not necessary to the goals and objectives of the survey initiative, the design team needs seriously to consider deleting them or saving them for a future assessment. These days more than ever, time is a precious commodity for people in organizations and they do not look favourably on others who waste theirs. When a survey is perceived as being too lengthy and time-consuming, it can create not only a very negative opinion of the survey itself but also of the corporate initiative to which it has been tied, the usefulness of surveys in general, and even the company as a whole. In addition, we have heard many people in organizations say that they are feeling 'surveyed to death', these days. Remember that odds are your assessment tool is probably not the only one they are being asked to complete. It is good survey practice to take this into account when constructing and administering your instrument.

Avoid double-barrelling

It is necessary not only to keep the survey relatively short and simple, but also to make sure that the individual items themselves are clear and uncomplicated. One of the most common mistakes made in item construction is attempting to measure more than one idea at a given time. This type of item design problem is referred to as being double-barrelled. Most survey practitioners at one time or another have used questions of this nature even though it is probably the biggest survey 'no-no' in the book. Double-barrelled items are usually the result of an effort to reach a design compromise or get the biggest 'bang for your buck' in terms of the total number of concepts measured in the survey. The interpretation of the data collected using this type of item is uncertain at best, and it may prove relatively useless and unsatisfying. On the other hand, there are some cases where the data gathered from this type of item are not as much of a problem for those people working with the data, particularly where the assessment in question is highly attitudinal in nature from the start. Again, these types of problematic items can often be avoided through group process checks, quality control and appropriate attention to the testing process. It also helps to have an objective third party proofread your items particularly with regard to this specific double-barrelling issue. Examples of commonly used items that seek to measure more than one construct are:

1. To what extent are you satisfied with your salary and benefits?
2. To what extent do employees support the mission and vision of company XYZ?
3. To what extent does your manager earn the trust and respect of employees?
4. To what extent does your manager coach and mentor people in new assignments?

The concepts presented are similar in each of these sample items (e.g., between mission and vision in question 1 or trust and respect in question 3), but they are not the same. Because of politics and personal agendas, however, the use of these types of questions is commonplace. These items should be used sparingly, if at all.

Be clear and concise

It is better to be clear and concise with a survey item than long-winded and obtuse. Simple enough in concept, this is often difficult to accomplish in practice. Words and phrases that are clear to one person or group are often obscure or out of context to another.

Consider carefully and understand the respondent group or audience that will ultimately be surveyed when developing survey items. Factors such as the target group's educational background, reading level and whether or not English is a first or second language must be taken into account. The best practice is to develop individual survey items with the lowest common denominator in mind. Making the items clear and simple will ensure greater readability and a more favourable translation into other languages if necessary. Practitioners should avoid the use of esoteric or uncommon words and/or expressions. In this way you can increase the likelihood that the majority of the survey respondent group will have little or no difficulty in completing the survey. A good way to combat threats to readability and the likelihood of inappropriate language is to test the survey with a diverse group. Outside proofreaders are also recommended.

Similarly, the use of jargon in surveys or questionnaires should be avoided wherever and whenever possible. In particular, jargon that is culturally specific to a nation, an industry or an ethnicity can be very confusing and frustrating to people of different backgrounds. For instance, instead of asking 'To what extent do team members work toward win-win solutions', one should ask 'To what extent do team members work towards mutually satisfying outcomes'. Likewise, rather than trying to measure the 'value-add' of an intervention or approach, it is probably better to measure its 'contribution'.

Another source of confusion is negatively worded items. An example of this would be 'To what extent are employees demotivated to do their jobs effectively?' We have heard many practitioners and survey sponsors advocate the inclusion of a few of these types of items because they think the change in format will make the respondent really 'think about their answer'; however, in our experience these types of questions instead represent a significant source of confusion and frustration. They are difficult for respondents to rate and are equally difficult to describe when working with the survey feedback. At the very least they must be reverse scored for analysis purposes, which assumes that the scale in reverse is comparable to the other scales used in the survey in their original form. When these types of items are used only a few times in a survey instrument they often go unnoticed by respondents who have a certain response in mind, based in large part on the understanding of the response scales used throughout the rest of the instrument. Because of this, participants respond in a manner exactly opposite to that which they had intended. These items often

59

have to be removed from the final reporting process because they are potentially invalid and difficult to work with.

Unfortunately, it is not always easy to be clear and concise in one's item writing style, nor is it simple to assess the quality of an instrument on one's own. For example, we were in a client meeting discussing our progress on a new survey draft. One of the participants, who was not one of the survey design team members, voiced her concern that there was too much ambiguity in some of the items. After the meeting was over the survey team reconvened without this individual and debriefed the meeting. We were all wondering what had happened. At the time of their initial construction, the items had seemed perfectly clear to us. We had spent so much time and effort working together, participatively and supportively, to craft the items contained on this new draft that we thought we had achieved synergy and a sense of team spirit. Instead we had obviously confused and disappointed this particular individual. After some discussion someone in the group chimed in, 'Well, you know what they say, a camel is a horse created by a committee'. This brings us back to the idea that sometimes groups working together can fall prey to their own ineffective processes. In the spirit of collaboration, and everyone putting in their two pennyworth, we created a draft survey instrument that to this outside reader was unclear and muddled. As a result, we had to review the entire questionnaire and its relationship to the project objectives, and then examine the individual items piece by piece to make sure that each of the issues assessed was clearly worded and distinct from one another.

Avoid leading and biased questions

This might seem like common sense, but remember to avoid constructing survey items that are either overly leading or biased towards a certain response by design. Survey items should provide an appropriate range of options and the wording of the item itself should be made to be as free of value judgements as possible. The inherent interests of the survey sponsor and/or various key constituent groups are likely to be evident to the respondents at a relatively broad level (e.g., a survey on the interest in various benefits options is probably related to an initiative of the human resources function), the less the specific items themselves show the preferred responses the better.

For example, the question below reflects the general assumption that senior leadership is overpaid:

To what extent do you think the senior leadership of your organization is overpaid?

①	②	③	④	⑤	⑩ⓚ
To a very small extent		To a moderate extent		To a very great extent	

Although this may indeed be the case, by phrasing the question in this manner the respondent is (a) forced to agree with this sentiment to a very small extent at least, even if he or she feels that the statement is not true at all, (b) is reminded of the pay disparity issue, which might negatively affect the remainder of the items to be rated following this one, and (c) is given the subtle message, presumably endorsed by the survey sponsor, that senior leaders are overpaid. A better item reflecting the same type of content might read:

With respect to pay, senior leadership is

① ② ③ ④ ⑤ (DK)

very underpaid   fairly paid   very overpaid

Ensure item–scale agreement

The final principle of good survey item design concerns the extent to which the item stem used matches the scale options provided. We have paid significant attention to the type of question, scale options and specific issues and pitfalls when phrasing new items, however, regardless of the format or content the item should be internally consistent. This is another relatively simple idea in concept, but in practice it is quite easy to confuse or obscure the response options by adding too many additional and/or unrelated scale descriptors. For example, the question below regarding value placed on employees ranges from not being valued or respected to being treated well (whatever that means to the respondent):

To what extent does company XYZ value its employees?

① ② ③ ④ ⑤

To a small extent –   To a very
employees are not   great extent – employees
valued or respected   are treated well

These two options neither match each other or the item stem. One of the simplest ways to correct many of these inconsistencies is to ensure that the only words used in the ends of the scale are those taken from the stem of the item itself. Additional outside readers and testing also help a great deal.

PRE-TEST THE SURVEY

The last step in the survey design process consists of pre-testing the survey with a real group of respondents. This is the 'acid test' as to whether or not the instrument that has been so painstakingly designed is clear, understandable and

Table 2.9   Sample test survey questionnaire

Purpose of the questionnaire

You have been chosen as one of 200 employees who are being asked to participate in a pilot test of the enclosed company XYZ survey. Your participation will help refine this survey for use throughout your organization and is therefore very important.

This questionnaire is designed to give senior leadership in your company feedback from employees on important issues facing your organization today. Over the past few months, a sample of employees has been queried on this matter both in interviews and focus group meetings. The key themes which have emerged have been translated into this survey which you are being asked to complete. It should only take 30 to 60 minutes of your time. When completing the survey please consider its usability in terms of the following criteria as you will be asked to evaluate this survey after you have completed it:

Clarity – are the instructions and items easy to read?
Relevance – are the items meaningful to you?
Specificity – are the items detailed or are they too general in nature?

Please be frank in responding to this questionnaire. This information will be of little value unless you provide as accurate an evaluation as you can. Your responses will remain completely confidential. Under no circumstances will your ratings be released to others in your organization. The data will be analysed by an outside contractor.

Instructions: please answer the following questions

1. How long did it take you to complete the questionnaire? Circle your response.

    a) Less than 30 minutes
    b) Between 30 minutes and 1 hour
    c) Between 1 and 1 1/2 hours
    d) Over 1 1/2 hours

2. What were your general reactions to the survey? (Please write in the space below.)

    a) Very negative
    b) Negative
    c) No reaction/neutral
    d) Positive
    e) Very positive

3. What were your reactions to the covering letter and instructions (e.g., was the intent of the effort clearly communicated)?

4. Please list any items that were difficult to answer and specify reasons using the list below:

    a) Unclear
    b) Not relevant to my work site
    c) Too general in scope – hard to rate

5. Did the response scale (1 To a very small extent to 5 To a very great extent) provide you with enough choices in making your ratings?

6. What themes or areas, in your opinion, received either too much or not enough coverage (in terms of items)?

    Areas covered too much:
    Areas not covered enough:
    Areas not covered at all:

7. Are there any other issues, concerns or suggestions you would like to raise to help improve the survey?

---

comprehensive with respect to what it purports to measure. The pre-test process is often one of the first elements to be curtailed when project timing begins to slip and timelines are readjusted, the fact is that the pre-test is really one of the few legitimate places where problems and issues inherent in the survey tool can be identified and resolved before they cause significant damage to the overall survey effort. It is often the only phase where people not directly involved in the planning, development and construction process have an opportunity to provide their relatively unbiased input.

When pre-testing a survey instrument the respondents should assess the content of the questionnaire itself according to the following three criteria:

1. Clarity: are the instructions and items easy to read and understand?
2. Relevance: are the items meaningful to the participant?
3. Specificity: are the items sufficiently detailed or are they too general in nature?

It is useful to query participants about these three components of the survey through the use of a 'pre-test survey questionnaire'. This survey-within-a-survey asks them to rate the larger instrument on these three basic dimensions. It also allows for other types of information and/or hypotheses to be gathered and tested as well (e.g., assessing differences in content layout and item ordering, using extra numbers of items with the intent of reducing a certain number, determining the average length of time needed to complete the tool, etc.). Table 2.9 provides a sample instrument of this type that has been used in an actual pre-test survey assessment project.

Results from this type of test assessment provide the survey practitioner and the survey design team with invaluable information about the draft document beyond the standard means, standard deviations ranges and missing data frequencies associated with a pre-test of only the survey tool itself. In combination, this information should be used to guide the survey design team in making the necessary modifications to the style, content and language of the final instrument. The objective nature of the pre-test data (assuming the test was conducted with a group of individuals not associated with the survey project), is also useful in helping survey team members construct an instrument free of their own biases and create a survey that is truly customer driven. At this stage, the survey team should have a completed assessment tool that has been well tested and is ready for the next phase of the survey process – administration.

CHECKLIST FOR STEP 2

Use a survey design team to build a better survey:

- Convene or assemble a survey design team.

- Involve strategically placed, highly visible and credible members of management.
- Involve technical and conceptual experts.

1. Gather preliminary information about important issues.

2. Identify key issues by summarizing and integrating all sources of information.

3. Discuss your findings with those who gave you input.

4. Draft the initial survey document based on your agreed key issues. Consider the following:
   - survey length
   - number of items per content area
   - number of response options
   - unipolar versus bipolar response options
   - the key issues
   - parsimony
   - avoid double-barrelling
   - clarity of wording
   - avoid leading and biased questions
   - ensure item–scale agreement.

5. Pre-test the survey with your representative group and other organizational members.

3 Communicating objectives

What we've got here is failure to communicate.

Frank R. Pierson

Communication is one of the primary means by which people structure themselves into the social systems that we call work. Without the ability to communicate, contemporary organizations as we know them would cease to exist (Katz and Kahn, 1978). Communication is something we do all the time, everyday, in our personal and professional lives. We often take this process for granted (both with others in our immediate work setting as well as systematically within the rest of the organization and even beyond its boundaries), but it is our *ability* to communicate that allows us to co-ordinate and collaborate our actions, make important decisions that affect more than one individual at a time, and ultimately function as an organizational entity. Whatever else changes either in the external environment or internal to the organization – e.g., leadership, management, organizational structure, team-based reward systems – communication will always remain the glue that holds together different functions, groups and individuals.

We all know what can happen when people communicate poorly: messages can be confused, misunderstood, misinterpreted, or even altered in various ways when being transferred from individual to individual or from group to group. Communicating effectively with others, particularly when the messages are complex in nature, is rarely as easy as it is made out to be. Differences in people's perspectives also add to this quagmire of complexity.

For example, we were involved in a large-scale survey of the administrative staff of a large, prestigious, world-renowned academic institution. After several meetings with our client, and our client's supervisor, we conducted an initial focus group with 15 senior HR personnel and staff members from different areas to determine the main issues that were facing the organization. Before the meeting could get under way, however, the topic of discussion turned to the specific intent of the survey effort as detailed in the official covering letter being

65

sent to employees. These participants refused to proceed with a discussion of the issues until they were comfortable with the purpose of the survey and the message that was being given to employees regarding this purpose. These concerns are perfectly understandable and legitimate, but we had been led to believe that this group was already 'on board' with the survey effort and were aware of the project plan and intent. However, all they knew was that a survey was in the works for some undisclosed reason. Needless to say, it produced a significant amount of anxiety that had to be dealt with and managed before the discussion of important issues could begin. When we challenged our client regarding this issue, she responded with 'I don't want them to know too much'. Had the communication process been more open with these senior-level staff personnel in HR, the focus group would have gone smoother and been better received, which in turn could have benefited the survey effort by generating greater commitment and support among this group. Instead, there was probably a greater level of resentment and suspicion generated than was necessary. And all this was among a group of only 15 people. Imagine the impact if a survey had been simply dropped on some lower-level employee's desk without any significant information regarding its objectives and intended uses! The effect could have been enough to defeat the assessment process before it even started.

Effective communication is a necessary ingredient for all types of organizations and organizational initiatives, and for the success of organizational survey efforts. We have already touched on the importance of effective communication, particularly in the initial phases of the survey development and project planning process, but we have yet to consider the key aspects of communication as it specifically relates to the survey roll-out process to end users – i.e., employees. This step discusses some of the key issues that are part of this process. First, however, a better understanding of the general nature of organizational communication is required. This will be achieved through a brief introduction and overview to the CPR model of organizational communication (Church, 1994b, 1996). Based on an integration of theoretical approaches taken from social psychology, management science and sociology – e.g., systems theory, information processing models, and symbolic interactionism – the CPR model provides a simple yet effective means of both integrating and advancing our understanding of how communication actually works in organizations. It is through this approach to understanding the levels of communication in organizations that effective survey communication efforts can be facilitated.

THE CPR MODEL OF ORGANIZATIONAL COMMUNICATION

Many people talk about the *supportive* nature of communication in relation to the success of various organizational initiatives such as an organization assessment survey, however in practice this important element is often considered only as a background or contextual variable. This is true, despite the fact that the context of 'good' communication – usually described as a combination of being open, honest, participative or direct with others – has been recognized by total quality management (TQM), HRD and OD practitioners as being one of the corner-stones of the successful implementation of *any* large organizational change initia-tive (Beckhard and Pritchard, 1992; Burke and Jackson, 1991; Sashkin and Kiser, 1993), including survey efforts (e.g., Kraut, 1996a).

Arguably the first step in improving organizational communication efforts is a firm understanding of how this process works in a given organizational setting. The CPR model of communication (Church, 1994b, 1996) is a simple yet effect-ive framework for understanding the basic issues and levels of communication in a organizational system. By using this model, one can gain a better under-standing of the three key components of organizational communication and some of the interrelationships that describe its character and function. These consist of:

- the *what* that is communicated (content)
- *how* it is communicated (processes)
- *who* does the communicating (roles).

Organizational communication can be conceptualized and understood using three primary dimensions: content, processes and roles. Each of these elements has been derived from existing theory and research. Figure 3.1 depicts these three factors and their relationships. The outer circle encompassing the model represents the permeable boundaries of the *primary system of focus*. This reflects the highest level of analysis to which the model is being applied – i.e., the entire organization or organizational unit being assessed in the survey effort.

The triangular image of the model depicts the causal relationships among the three dimensions. Content, located at the top of the triangle, is the single most important dimension to consider when trying to understand the character and function of communication process in a given organizational system. Processes and roles are located at the bottom of the triangle. Without an understanding of the nature of the survey content itself, it is virtually impossible to grasp either the preferred method of transmission (process) throughout the organization, or what groups or individuals (roles) are responsible for and/or involved in making this transfer of information occur. For a given survey effort, it is important first to understand the objectives and goals of the survey process before determining

67

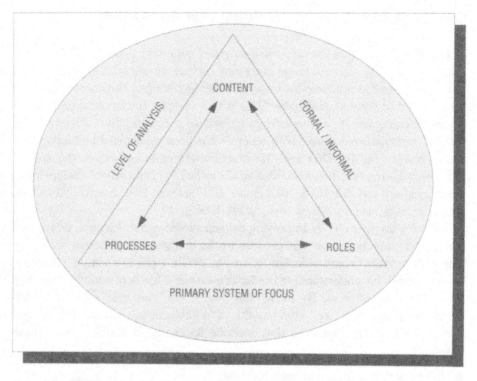

Figure 3.1   The CPR model of organizational communication
Reproduced by permission: MCB University Press and International Journal of Organizational Analysis

the best means of communicating these to respondents and key stakeholders in the organization.

The two arrows pointing from content to processes and roles in Figure 3.1 reflect this differential level of importance. However, since both processes and roles can also positively or negatively impact the nature of the message being communicated, the arrows also point up from these two dimensions, indicating this reciprocal relationship. The arrows connecting processes to roles reflect their *interdependent* nature.

Taking each of these three aspects of communication separately, the C in the CPR model refers to the actual *content* of the communication exchange, or the *what* that is being communicated. The information we are referring to here will provide answers to the following types of questions: What are the key messages to be communicated regarding the survey effort? Why is the survey being conducted? Who is responsible for the survey effort? What types of issues are they interested in asking me? What is the expected time frame with respect to when I can see some results? What is the commitment to action based on the data collected? If the basic content message of the survey is either weak or unclear, it will have a significant impact on the perceived utility and subsequently the outcome of the entire process. This is why, as we have stated earlier, the content of the message itself is probably best thought of as the single most important element for approaching any type of organizational communication. Next, the arrows are directed downwards, affecting both the process and roles involved.

The second dimension or factor of the CPR model, P, describes the systemic *processes* of organizational communication. Included under this category are the mechanisms, methods, systems and patterns of interaction by which the actual content is implemented and/or transferred from one subsystem to another within the organization; that is to say, the *how* of organizational communication. Here the questions to ask regarding a survey initiative include: What are the key direct and indirect methods of communication to employees in this organization? By what means should the messages about the survey process be communicated? How do we ensure that we involve everyone who is going to be involved in the process? There is both a formal and an informal side to the processes dimension. Examples of formal processes include management information systems, computer networks, bulletin boards, forums, senior management presentations and company newsletters. The informal transfer mechanisms consist of meetings, social networks and contacts, and formal and informal reporting relationships. The key to choosing the most effective means of communicating to employees regarding survey efforts depends in large part on the nature of the existing processes. However, there are some general guidelines regarding survey-related communications which we will discuss later in this section.

This third factor in the CPR model refers to the *roles* and responsibilities of those individuals involved in the communication process. Remember that the role of the conveyor of information plays an important part in determining how information is presented and ultimately received. Here it is possible to identify exactly *who* – be it an individual, group or all members of the organization – is accountable for and/or otherwise involved in the selection, endorsement, establishment and maintenance of various communication processes *vis-à-vis* the survey effort. Issues here include: Who should write the cover letter and/or memos announcing the survey initiative and its intent? Who should be available (e.g., internal HR staff or independent external consultants) for calls and questions regarding the instrument during its administration? Who should provide the initial and follow-up reporting of results to individual unit heads in the organization? An important assumption of the CPR model is that in order to understand organizational communication fully you must examine the nature of the actors (or the roles that they inhabit) as well as the processes and the content of the situation. Of course, the focal point for these roles is determined first by the content of the information itself, and only then in relation to methods of its dissemination in the organization.

For example, to understand how a survey effort aimed at conveying information about a company's newly constructed mission and vision should be conducted, first become familiar with all the key messages that need to be communicated to employees regarding this mission and its importance to the organization. Next, the specific vehicles for delivering this message should be in alignment with prior communications regarding the mission and vision. For example, if a corporate news video was produced for the new mission and vision, it is probably appropriate to link the survey announcement with that same channel of distribution. Then the key players, in this case the most senior leaders of the organization, need to be included in the communication plan as well. On the other hand, a survey effort designed simply to assess people's opinion regarding the desirability of various possible options for a new personnel benefit programme is probably best handled by HR staff in conjunction with senior HR sponsorship, and through more direct lines of communication with people.

FIRST CONTACT WITH EMPLOYEES

With a firmer understanding of the basic aspects of organizational communication, we can now move to the process of first contact. As we discussed in Step 1, the first action in creating a successful survey effort is to generate clear, well-defined, achievable and measurable objectives. Once these elements have been put in place, and the content of the survey itself has been identified and delineated in the form of concrete questions, the people who will ultimately be responsible for providing the data must be brought up to speed as well.

This is achieved first through some form of initial or pre-communication, and then followed up through the administration of the actual survey instrument itself. If the objectives of the effort are unclear to the practitioners and/or the survey sponsor, they cannot be communicated to others. Rest assured, employees will know if a survey effort is being pushed on them without a clear purpose. Even in cases where there appears to be a relatively simple assessment plan for those initiating the survey effort, it is likely that other players in the organization will still want more detail regarding intended objectives and desired outcomes. In today's competitive and overworked business environment, time is a precious commodity, and a survey effort had better have a justifiable reason for infringing on people's time. For example, in many discussions with survey planning groups in organizations the question is often raised as to whether or not employees will be irritated by the additional time required (typically only 40 minutes to an hour in total) in completing a survey questionnaire. Thus, as we discussed in previous steps, gaining clarity of the content and purpose is crucial for obtaining support from employees. Assuming the goals of the effort have been well defined, however, let us start to outline a typical survey communication process.

We begin with the initial exposure to the concept of the assessment initiative. People need to be informed that the survey effort is forthcoming, well in advance of receiving the instrument itself. They need time to reflect on the importance of the survey effort and its relevance to their day-to-day experience. They also need to be clear about why the survey process has been initiated and *what to expect* from their contribution. If a survey is simply distributed without warning – e.g., dropped on people's desks one morning – the initial reaction is likely to be one of suspicion or frustration, as in the examples described above, rather than interest and excitement. In the absence of knowledge, the assumption is often that 'senior management must be hiding something, otherwise they would have let us know this was coming'. While it is not always possible to predict employees' reactions to the idea of doing a survey, even with a carefully orchestrated survey communication effort, strong negative responses are particularly likely in organizations where fear and mistrust are rife – a not uncommon situation in contemporary organizations highly experienced with downsizing and related staff reduction plans. Employees, or others to whom the instrument is to be distributed, should be well informed in advance about the survey process and its intent.

The process for conducting this initial communication can be facilitated in many different ways. Each format or method of delivering information to employees has its associated positives and negatives. Table 3.1 provides an overview of the differences among three commonly used modes of communicating survey messages.

Table 3.1   Differences in communication methods

Corporate communication (e.g., video, newsletter)	Letter to employees	E-mail to employees
formal	formal	informal
group approach	individual approach	individual approach
flexible amount of detail	requires more detail	requires more detail
moderate cost	moderate cost	low cost
variable reach	full reach	variable reach
high political factor	moderate political factor	moderate political factor
delayed delivery	delayed delivery	quick delivery
no direct reply	no direct reply	ability to reply
complex effort	moderate effort	moderate effort

The best option for any given organization is probably dependent on the type and style of communication process currently in place. For example, in an organization where the company newsletter or newspaper is a highly read and appreciated vehicle, it might be appropriate to run a full feature article on the upcoming survey effort. In these circumstances, information such as the origins of the initiative, the intended objectives, the intended time frame (from administration through to the delivery of results and action planning), issues of confidentiality – i.e., who will get to see the data and in how much detail – and the content and types of issues need to be assessed. Of course, this means that the timing of this communication may have to be co-ordinated with the existing publication and production schedules of the in-house newspaper system unless a special edition is pursued.

Other organizations, both large and small, prefer using a formal letter from the CEO, the head of human resources or some similarly high-placed senior manager (e.g., the champion of the survey effort) to convey the intent of the survey effort. These more formal letters or memos cover the same issues but in a more direct one-to-one exchange with each employee (particularly if mailed to their home address rather than through internal mail at work). Unless the company is very small and/or very informal, a letter addressed to each employee from the CEO regarding the survey effort can be a very powerful form of communication. Still other companies have used corporate-wide e-mail, small postcards with a survey or other corporate 'initiative'-related logos and slogans, and/or internal television programming as other means of conveying their message. Smaller organizations often rely on word of mouth or direct contact with senior individuals on site. It all depends on the nature of the organization and the types of process and roles that comprise its total communication system.

COMMUNICATING THE SURVEY ITSELF

Once the initial contact regarding the survey effort has been made, employees are left waiting for the final product – i.e., the actual instrument itself. Some time is needed between the first message and the survey administration in order to soften the impact and initial level of resistance associated with the assessment process, but this delay often leads to increased anxiety and apprehension on the part of employees. They begin to doubt the messages originally provided, particularly in organizations where trust is lacking. Therefore, regardless of the resting state of the organization, it is necessary to have a strong, well-defined second level of communication provided with the survey instrument itself. Often this takes the form of a covering letter from senior management and/or an introductory section to the instrument that delineates to the user once again the key

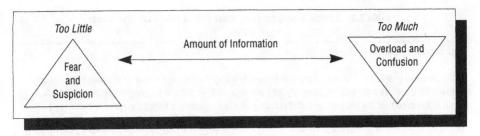

Figure 3.2   Balancing the right amount of information

messages of the survey regarding purpose, item coverage and, above all else at this stage, the confidentiality of the data to be obtained.

People want and need to know what the survey effort is all about. They do not need to know all the details of its construction, or those of the vendor selection process or why certain individuals are supporting the survey and others are not. It is extremely important to provide information about the general intentions of the survey effort; however, the quality and level of detail must be tempered to meet the needs of the specific audience. If a full feature story is being produced about the assessment project in the company newspaper, then more detailed information can probably be provided. The covering letter and survey instructions need to be accurate and complete, but not overly complex and/or inscrutable. The idea here is to let respondents know why the survey is in their hands, why it is important to their day-to-day jobs, why they should participate and what will happen afterwards. Too little information fails to provide key messages; too much detail can obscure them. Figure 3.2 gives an overview of this dynamic.

It may seem relatively straightforward to compose a simple covering letter for a survey; however, there are a number of subtle issues that should be addressed in order to ensure that the messages have been communicated clearly and effectively. The decision to include a covering letter from a senior ranking official in the organization can be an important one, particularly if the use of surveys is either new or has a negative history in the organization. Having the effort endorsed by the board of directors, a new CEO or the head of human resources, sends a clear signal to respondents that someone important is behind the initiative and has taken the time and effort to encourage people to respond. Your internal client may want to be the one to write and sign the covering letter, but this person may not be the most appropriate figurehead for gathering support for and commitment to the effort. This can become a political issue at times as people's private agendas are likely to become involved in some level of the planning effort (as discussed in Step 1), nevertheless the survey effort must receive

73

Table 3.2   Sample survey covering letter from a chief executive officer

---

Dear Survey Respondent,

In the past two years, we've come a long way toward fulfilling the Promise of our organization. Yet, much needs to be done. As a member of company XYZ management, you share a strong interest in and deserve much of the credit for the success of our continuing efforts in building a better company.

This survey is another tool in those efforts. Its purposes are 1) to obtain your views on 'how we are doing' at company XYZ in such key areas as leadership, teamwork, job satisfaction, overall effectiveness and others; and 2) to establish a data 'bench mark' so that we will be able to compare how we are doing over time. In short, I believe this kind of information will allow us to make the continuous improvements so important to our ongoing business.

Be assured that all responses will be summarized by an outside contractor, and individuals will remain completely anonymous. Both results and separate business reports will be available later in the year.

Please complete and return your questionnaire in the enclosed envelope, or as directed by your General Manager. Thank you for your prompt and thoughtful response.

Sincerely,

Ure Leeder

Chief Executive Officer

---

appropriate sponsorship and credibility from a recognized, senior source in the organization. Table 3.2 provides a sample covering letter from a recent survey effort, written by the CEO of a multinational corporation, that was mailed to the entire management staff (approximately 4,800 individuals).

If we look closely at the letter in Table 3.2, it does indeed cover many of the issues and topics discussed. For example, there is a clear reference to existing organizational initiatives and progress already made to date (the word 'promise' was capitalized to reflect another corporate-wide programme). The survey is then positioned as a part of this ongoing process as a tool for building a better company. Notice there is no hint of negative consequences (e.g., downsizing or finger-pointing) as a result of the survey effort. The emphasis is on obtaining management views regarding a specific set of content areas and establishing a bench mark for the future. There is a reference to the external protection provided by an outside consulting firm with respect to the confidentiality of the individual survey results, as well as an indication (albeit somewhat vague) of when the results of the survey process can be expected and in what forms. This information could just as easily be woven into the introductory pages of a survey (see

74

Table 3.3   Sample survey covering letter from a unit/department head

Dear Colleague,

Here is the questionnaire for the 1996/97 staff survey. As with the first survey in 1995, we want to know your views on the future direction of XYZ, the way that it is managed and how you feel about many aspects of your job and working environment.

The questionnaire should take about 50 minutes to complete. I have asked your managers to give you a chance to complete this questionnaire during work time. We want you to be frank and honest about your opinions and in return we guarantee complete confidentiality. No one in XYZ will see your responses and the way the results are reported will prevent anyone's responses from being identified.

In addition, each member of the management team will be given the results for their own department. This will help them to consider what their staff have strong views about and where improvements can be made. This means that your views count for your department and the unit as well as XYZ as a whole, and you will be able to see the results at each of these levels.

I will act on the 1996/97 staff survey results. Between March and April your manager will discuss the department results with you and decide how each department will deal with the issues raised. The unit management team will then decide what we should be tackling throughout the entire unit. I will then take some of your suggestions to the senior management board of XYZ. Later, when the XYZ-wide results are published, you will hear the board's response and their plans for the whole organization.

Everyone who works at XYZ can contribute, directly or indirectly, to making an excellent product. Becoming a better managed organization is central to this. Please help us make this happen in our business unit and the organization as a whole by filling in the questionnaire. Your views are important and your help is appreciated.

Thank You

Linus Q. Managere

Unit Head

Table 3.3 for an example of this type of approach), but the impact of having it presented in a stand-alone memo from the CEO was enough to generate significantly better than expected returns (73 per cent of all management) for this first survey effort in this organization. Given the high degree of uncertainty present in the company at the time, due in large part to a recent post-merger situation, the level of involvement in and commitment to the survey effort was indeed a positive surprise.

Sometimes, the letter accompanying a survey effort can be very effective when it comes from the local-level senior manager – i.e., the person with line authority over a business unit. In more decentralized organizations, such as the one from which the sample in Table 3.3 originates, if the individual in that position presents a strong and visible image, the key messages regarding the survey effort can be even more effective coming from this source. As you can see, there are many similarities between this covering letter and the one from the CEO presented in Table 3.2, but there are also some clear differences. Most notably, because of the more direct nature of this individual's position in the business unit, he or she was able to make much more specific commitments to employees regarding the timing and outcomes of the survey effort. The letter is clear in its message that this survey effort is important enough to warrant time spent on its completion by employees during work hours – an issue that is often hotly debated in the planning phase and one that many organizations are not willing to commit to upholding (even if it has been agreed in policy).

Table 3.4 shows yet another example of introductory survey communication – this time a statement of purpose – taken from an actual instrument used in a large financial organization. This message to all respondents represents the

Table 3.4   Sample survey introduction

This survey is intended to establish a baseline measurement for determining our progress towards our strategic plan. It will also serve as a starting point for making improvements to our business. Your participation in the survey is very important, so please take the time to complete it.

The questions in the survey concern your business unit as well as the entire organization. The questions cover many aspects of the organization and are intended to measure progress in key areas of performance, leadership, customer service and employee satisfaction.

With the exception of the write-in comments included at the end, please answer all questions on the Response Form provided. The questionnaire form has a total of 100 questions for you to complete.

Each question is rated on a 5-point scale, with '1' and '5' reflecting the opposite ends of the scale. Please consider the full range between 1 and 5 in making your response. Each statement should be answered according to your own experience and opinion, and should reflect your perception of present overall conditions.

Space is provided at the end of the survey for any comments you may have. These comments will be transcribed and grouped with others according to common themes as a part of the survey results analysis.

An external firm will process these questionnaires. *Your individual responses will not be released to anyone in company XYZ.* This survey is completely confidential. After scoring, your answer sheet and write-in commentary sheet will be destroyed.

Survey results will be communicated to senior management and then immediately reported to all employees in a special edition of the company's newsletter. Then senior executives and business unit heads will integrate this information into their yearly action plans. You will have the opportunity to discuss the survey results with your manager and business unit head.

When you have completed the questionnaire, seal your Response Form and write-in comments page in the return envelope provided. If you have any questions regarding the completion of the survey, please contact the output of several focus group sessions designed to set the key objectives of the survey, as well as planning meetings with the survey development team and our client. You will notice that compared with the letters from the CEO and unit head presented above, this sample includes (a) more detail regarding the nature of the item formats and layout, and (b) a greater emphasis on the confidentiality of the data and what will happen to raw responses after they have been tallied, but (c) is less well crafted with respect to conveying key messages about the survey's intent as well as likely outcomes.

GUIDELINES FOR COMMUNICATING TO EMPLOYEES

Now that we have covered the two types of preparatory communications related to a survey effort, we shall summarize briefly the specific types of information that need to be covered. There are several simple guidelines that exist with respect to the communication to employees regarding a survey effort. Most of these have been alluded to above, but they are important enough to reiterate more specifically here:

1. Provide an adequate amount of advanced notice regarding the survey effort as well as at the time of its administration
2. Provide as much information as possible concerning the survey effort without overloading people with excessive detail
3. Convey the key messages involved clearly and effectively
4. Use multiple methods and processes to reinforce the same messages (e.g., letter from senior management, reminders in the company newsletter, e-mail messages, postcard reminders, etc.)
5. Convey honesty and openness in approach: surveys are a participative, voluntary data-gathering process, not a mandated directive
6. Highlight the sponsorship, roles and various levels of participation in the survey among key organizational members
7. Involve the highest and most credible level of formal support available for a given group (e.g., the CEO for an entire organization, the unit head for an entire function, etc.)
8. Make a commitment to action as a result of the survey and when it can be expected.

People need to know as much as possible about the survey effort so that they can take it seriously and understand its relationship to their everyday work life, otherwise the survey is just another boring assessment effort that will have no impact and is therefore not worth participating in, or worse, is seen as an unknown and highly feared instrument in which people will alter their responses in attempts to second guess its true purpose. During survey efforts some practitioners try to hide key information (e.g., regarding objectives), because they either feel that employees will not 'appropriately' understand the effort, or they have some additional set of agenda that they (a) do not want to be made public or (b) do not want to commit to fully unless certain conditions are met. For example, in one survey initiative in which we were involved, we were working closely with our client in human resources developing the survey instrument. In fact, we were very close to putting the finishing touches to our survey document, when, seemingly out of the blue, we heard from our client that a member of the CEO's staff wanted to meet with us regarding the survey. We were informed – to our amazement – that this individual had been totally unaware of the survey effort and its intent, and subsequently did not agree with many of the decisions that our client had already made and begun to implement. Human resources had gone ahead and decided to survey employees without checking first with the rest of senior management, let alone procuring their involvement. Needless to say, this presented us with some significant resistance, and we had to work on relationship management (as well as contract readjustment) before the survey effort could move forward.

Those organizations that find it difficult to openly communicate key messages to their employees are often likely to have other related issues emerge during the survey implementation and feedback process as well. These are often the same projects, for example, in which issues of confidentiality and mistrust are raised later in the process once the data have been collected. Because it is not always possible to identify these situations before they occur, it is best to try to get the survey sponsor to publicly identify his or her goals and stance regarding confidentiality of data. As with the idea of generating measurable objectives, by having the sponsor state his or her position on issues of data confidentiality and use the organization at a later date can support the integrity of the effort beyond just the practitioner's personal ethics. However, this is often, a risky proposition because it amounts to getting the client to agree to make a very public commitment as to his or her intended approach. It is also, of course, one of the few ways to ensure honesty and follow-through amid a sea of political pressures and demands that are often issued after the initial presentation of results (more on this issue in Steps 5 and 6).

RECOGNIZING INFORMAL SYSTEMS

Prior to the next stage of the survey process – i.e., the administration – we need to say a few words about the power and potential impact of informal methods of communication during a survey effort. To understand fully and utilize the formal means of communication in an organizational system as we have discussed at length in this section is very important; however, the role of the informal processes must also be recognized. These informal methods can have a significant effect on any type of organizational initiative, particularly if they are used extensively as a means of communicating among employees. For example, in a company where fear and distrust of management is strong, messages transmitted by word of mouth can damage the entire survey process – regardless of whether or not those messages are correct.

But is this a problem? How much do employees rely on informal as opposed to formal modes of communicating anyway? The answers to these questions most certainly lie in the specific configuration of the organization in question, nevertheless we do have some data that speak to this issue. Let us take an actual example. In a recent survey effort designed to measure corporate culture conducted in a large publicly funded organization in the UK, the internal corporate communications function asked us to include a relatively comprehensive section in the survey instrument regarding the extent to which different communication processes or mechanisms provided information to employees. Figure 3.3 shows a display of the results of this question based on responses from approximately 4,500 employees across all levels of management.

Despite the hard work and good intentions of the communication staff, it was apparent that employees in this organization relied most heavily on the grapevine for their information about what was going on in the organization. The next best source for these employees was the external coverage of their organization by the media (not unexpected in this organizational setting, given the nature of their business and their high degree of visibility to the public), followed by discussions with their immediate manager or supervisor. Corporate publications, letters and memos and e-mail – all of which were discussed above as potential outlets for formal survey-related communications – were only moderately effective (above a 3.0 on the rating scale) and by no means the most frequently relied on source. In this organization the informal methods were just as important, if not more so, as the formal ones for providing information. Not surprisingly, as a result of these findings, changing employees' perceptions of the relevance, timeliness and importance of corporate communications became one of the future initiatives of the communications function.

Regardless of one's efforts, these types of informal methods of exchange will always exist in organizations. They cannot be removed or diverted. All that practitioners can do is (a) make efforts to enhance the perceptions of the formal internal communication process, and/or (b) try to find ways to use the informal mechanisms to one's advantage to reinforce the appropriate messages regarding various development and improvement efforts. Once again, this brings us to recommend the use of multiple parallel messages regarding a survey effort

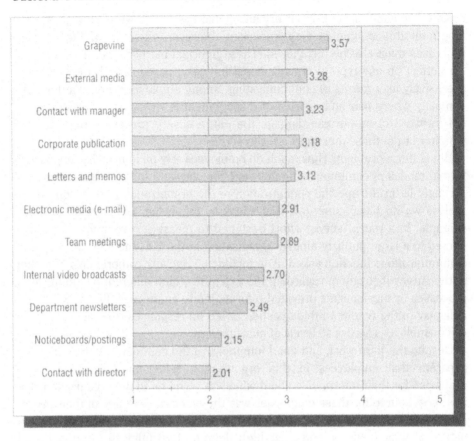

Figure 3.3 Effectiveness of various communication mechanisms in XYZ

wherever possible. The most important aspect to remember about the role of communication in organizational surveys is that the messages provided reflect and reinforce people's perceptions of the quality, importance, relevance and meaningfulness of the entire intervention and/or corporate initiative to which it has been linked. Therefore, extreme care is required when preparing and planning for a survey effort.

CHECKLIST FOR STEP 3

1. Remember the CPR model of organizational communication.
   - Determine *what* will be communicated (Content).
   - Determine *how* it will be communicated (Processes).
   - Determine *who* will do the communicating (Roles).

2. Communicate with employees beforehand.
   - Generate clear, well-defined, achievable and measurable objectives well in advance of the survey.
   - Consider the positives and negatives associated with different modes of communication (e.g., letter to employees, e-mails, videos).
   - Follow up with the administration of the survey instrument itself.

3. Consider the following guidelines for effective communication:
   - Provide an adequate amount of advanced notice regarding the survey effort.
   - Give as much information as possible without overloading people with excessive detail.
   - Convey the key messages involved clearly and effectively.
   - Use multiple methods and processes to reinforce the same messages.
   - Convey honesty and openness in approach.
   - Highlight sponsorship and roles among key organizational members.
   - Involve the highest and most credible level of formal support available.
   - Make a commitment to action as a result of the survey and when it can be expected.

4. Consider the impact of informal systems.

4   Administering the survey

> I have the consolation to reflect that during the period of my administration not a drop of the blood of a single fellow citizen was shed.
>
> Thomas Jefferson

Prior to the administration process, the task of designing an effective and impactful organizational survey has primarily been a cognitive one, full of planning, building interest and commitment, generating items that reflect key issues in the organization, and all the other elements that have been discussed to date. Now comes the legwork – the actual job of producing and distributing the assessment tool and gathering the responses for analysis. For some practitioners and in some organizational settings, this is the easy part. Just send out the surveys and wait for them to come back. In other organizations, however, this can be an extremely laborious, tedious and overly complex task. Sometimes it can prove to be very informative as well, particularly in those cases where the channels of distribution may not be as well known by the human resource functions as previously thought. We have seen a surprising number of survey efforts, for example, in which, as a result of the actual administration planning of the survey, the internal staff were unable to identify fully the entire organizational structure. This may seem odd at first but in large organizations, and particularly those undergoing restructuring efforts, it is not uncommon to find isolated units and functions after the survey effort is fully under way that were not included in the initial roll-out plan.

In most situations the actual administration of the survey is not the most important element to the success of the overall initiative; the attention to detail and level of complexity involved can play a crucial role in managing the quality and depth of the data collected as well as the entire image of the survey effort. The purpose of this step is to explore the issues involved in the survey administration process. Topics discussed include the key elements of survey timing, project planning, the pros and cons of various methods of administration and data collection, what to expect regarding response rates and how to use feedback from the process in real time to improve the survey effort.

TIMING OF ADMINISTRATION

One of the first questions asked about survey administration is when is the best time to survey people? Whenever organizations are embarking on a survey effort, it never seems to be the *right* time. Common reasons and/or excuses for this include 'We've just reorganized', 'We're just about to reorganize', 'We've just employed a new CEO', 'This is our busiest time', 'We are doing budgeting now'. The issue here, of course, is one of the anticipated reach of the survey effort (i.e., how many employees will receive the survey instrument and have enough time to complete it), and the resulting quantity and quality of the responses that are likely to be obtained. Timing is always a tough issue, yet there are definite windows of opportunity for each stage in the process and some times are better and worse than others. July and August, December and January, for example, are typically poor survey months, due to holiday schedules. People are not available to complete and return the instrument. On the other hand, early spring (e.g., March or April) and early autumn tend to be more successful times with respect to response rates and levels of receptivity. The only significant exception to this are organizations whose primary function is one of accounting or tax (e.g., professional service firms), in which case autumn is the best time.

Since the optimal amount of time to leave a survey open for responses is somewhere between one and two months, with most responses occurring early in the process, a survey can probably be successfully launched in May and early June. In this instance, July and August would be used primarily for the data analysis phase with an expected presentation roll-out in early September. In any case, the survey administration should be planned so that respondents feel that they have adequate time to complete and return the instrument. Similarly, the amount of time between the closing date for returns and the subsequent presentation of results must also be managed – the shorter this window the better (more on this topic in Steps 5 and 6). Always keep in mind, though, the survey objectives and linkages among the data collection effort itself and concurrent initiatives and/or processes occurring in the organization (e.g., annual budgeting, performance appraisals, training and development opportunities, pending changes in management positions, re-engineering efforts, formal structural relationships, or the launch of a formal culture change campaign, etc.). When the results of a survey effort are intended to be tied to one of these types of existing process, it is very important that the data be collected, analysed and reported back in time for its effective use. If a survey effort is intended to provide input into the annual performance management system of managers in various business units regarding managerial strengths and areas for improvement, for example, the data can be rendered useless if the survey results are not complete and in recipients' hands in time for the planning process. Timing decisions should be based in part on obtaining the best quantity and quality of responses possible, and administration dates must be made with a clear set of goals and targets in mind.

WORKING WITH THE PROJECT PLAN

A point that we have tried to make very clear throughout this book is the importance of having well-defined goals and objectives for any type of organizational survey effort. These help lead the practitioner through many of the early stages of survey design and into the analysis and action planning portions of the project. Just as these goals and objectives drive the entire survey process, there is a need for a clear, comprehensive and reasonable plan for the survey administration phase as well. In this case, however, rather than undertaking a series of more strategic objectives as outlined in Step 1, the plan must be very specific and detailed with respect to the following key elements:

- when the survey will be launched and when it will be closed
- the method by which the survey instrument is to be completed
- the respondents to whom the instruments are being distributed
- the means by which the instruments are going to be distributed
- the length of time respondents will have to complete and return the instrument
- the timing and types of additional information regarding the survey.

The survey administration plan also provides an opportunity to clarify the specific roles and responsibilities of each of the parties involved in the process. This includes everything from who does the printing and survey-packet mailing, to how the response tracking procedure will be conducted and the number of times the survey sponsor will receive updates. Table 4.1 provides a sample survey administration plan for a 3,500 census mail survey.

One of the first rules of thumb when preparing a survey administration plan is to realize that you cannot plan for everything. The practitioner should always expect the unexpected. This means that there need to be appropriate levels of slack or extra time built into the project timing so that last minute adjustments can be made. The sample plan in Table 4.1 does not specifically provide additional time in this regard, but because the timing is not tied to specific dates the entire process can be moved if necessary (e.g., if the printing process takes longer than expected). Other options might include making the survey-packet printing and preparation steps longer or perhaps including more time for the open administration period.

The survey administration plan needs to be relatively specific and clear, but it

85

Table 4.1   Sample survey administration plan

Task	Provider/role	Timing
Survey-packet printing/preparation		3 weeks
• Print 3,500 survey instruments	Printing vendor	
• 3,500 inner return envelopes with address pre-printed	Printing vendor	
• Print 3,500 optical scan response/answer sheets	Scanning vendor	
• 3,500 generic outer mailing envelopes	Stationery supplier	
• Provide employee home mailing address labels	HR staff	
Survey-packet assembly and external mailing		1 week
• Create 3,500 survey packets	Mailing vendor	
• Attach mailing labels	Mailing vendor	
• Frank outer envelopes, sort by postal code, distribute	Mailing vendor	
Internal administration option		1 week
• Assemble 500 additional packets without labels	Mailing vendor	
• Determine additional numbers and channels needed	HR staff	
• Distribution to internal staff as needed	Survey representatives	
Open response period		4 weeks
• Track and receive responses and optically scan to data file	Survey practitioner	
• Monitor response rates (daily)	Survey practitioner	
• Provide updates regarding response rates (weekly)	Survey practitioner	
• Compare incoming data to population data	Survey practitioner and HR staff	
• General follow-up	HR staff	
• Specific follow-up with non-respondents	HR staff	

must always have some manoeuvrability inherent in its design as well. There is almost always someone else who needs to be involved in the survey approval or communication process at the last minute, or some additional change that needs to be made to the instrument, covering letter or some other element. For example, we have seen a number of large-scale survey efforts, in which, only days from the initial administration, have suddenly been pulled from production to be re-examined and/or reworked (and occasionally even halted completely) by some other powerful group in the organization that had not been included or represented in the design process. This type of last minute intervention can be extremely problematic from a production standpoint as well as potentially damaging to the credibility and subsequent reliability of the survey effort. Consider, for example, a survey where the launch date has already been communicated to employees and then the survey is subsequently held for a few extra weeks. Of course, these kinds of issues can often be avoided with careful work at the start of the project. This is one of the reasons we have stressed the importance of involving the appropriate individuals in the survey design process in Steps 1 to 3.

Related to this issue is a simple rule of thumb regarding the use of administration dates. While the initial release date should be well communicated, the closing date for survey returns should be used (i.e., printed) sparingly throughout various documents and supporting materials so that if they do indeed change, as is often the case, there is less rework involved. For example, if you go ahead and print 4,000 copies of a custom survey return envelope with the closing date on the outside, and the survey is held up for any reason, the closing date will probably need to be shifted back, therefore making the already generated envelopes useless. These types of errors are common in organizations, and are often not very costly in the scheme of things; however, in this age of continuous improvement and better, faster, cheaper, it is better to avoid these kinds of wasteful occurrences whenever possible.

SAMPLE VERSUS CENSUS

One of the key decisions in the survey administration process, besides the issue of timing, is the nature of the respondent group. We alluded to this issue in Step 1 and indeed there should be some consideration of this in the survey plan, but it is in the administration phase that this issue must be ultimately resolved for it can affect both the overall size of the survey effort and the best means of distribution. More specifically, in survey work there is always a choice that must be made at some point before roll-out between conducting the survey using some sort of sample of employees or collecting data from the entire organization in a census effort. Both methods can suffer from some problems and biases as mentioned earlier with respect to instrument design and/or communication issues; however, there are some more specific pros and cons for each of these approaches. Table 4.2 provides a summary of the differences in assumptions and possible outcomes.

For the most part, the decision regarding a sample or census comes down to

Table 4.2   Sample versus census: a comparison

Sample	Census
• Smaller and easier to administer	• Larger and more complex to administer
• Less costly	• More costly
• Provides representative responses	• Provides complete responses
• Involves only certain employees	• Involves all employees
• Potential for sampling biases	• No sampling biases
• Easier to work with data	• More difficult to work with data
• Data analysis can be more limited	• Provides for greater depth in analyses
• Not appropriate for smaller organizations	• Should be used in smaller organizations

issues of cost and/or the complexity of the administration process. Sample surveys are easier and cheaper to conduct. In an organization where there is a shortage of time, money and staff, for example, a sample survey is often the only option. These are particularly useful when used between larger census administrations – e.g., as an interim assessment of improvement in a given area. Where the survey effort is fully supported by senior management and is part of the fabric of a much larger organization development and change initiative, a full-scale all-employee census is probably preferred. If one of the objectives of the survey process is to communicate some new set of corporate values or behaviours to employees, pursuing the census option is necessary as well. In such situations, the use of a sampling process is likely to result in (a) the dilution of the messages being communicated, (b) a decrease in employee commitment and perceived value of the survey effort, and (c) concerns regarding who was and was not included in the sample identified, and why (Paul and Bracken, 1995). Some practitioners have gone so far as to advocate against the use of sampling (e.g., Breisch, 1996), but this is often not practical from either a time or financial standpoint, particularly in large or very large organizations (e.g., 10,000 employees or more).

It is for these same reasons that the usage of sample surveys is popular in industry today. This is because, for the most part, if the sampling process is actioned correctly the data provided can be just as valid and reliable as that provided by a census. Conversely, a bad sampling process can introduce such significant biases as to at least skew the data in some specific direction, and at worst render the survey data totally useless. Thus, if a sample is warranted and/or required, the survey practitioner must have a firm understanding of sampling theory and all that is involved. This information is beyond the scope of this book, so we refer the interested reader to the following additional sources on sampling issues and construction: Frankel, 1983; Rea and Parker, 1997; Schuman and Kalton, 1985; Sudman, 1983. However, the primary concern in sampling is one of representation – i.e., does the sample used adequately reflect the demographic, functional and even dispositional makeup of the total population of interest? As the interested reader will see, there are a number of methods and approaches for generating samples that will indeed meet this criteria.

Beyond the potential for increased biases and involving fewer people in the assessment process, the only other significant limitation of a sample survey is an inability to provide more detailed cuts and/or analyses of the data based on the full range of demographic variables. A sample survey can provide an equally accurate snapshot of the total organization, and perhaps even some of its larger functions or regions, even with a 90 per cent response rate the sample will begin to fall short the lower the data is pushed. A full census, on the other hand, is limited in this regard only by the response rate. Since all employees were included, the potential is there to analyse the data and look for trends at the absolute lowest level (assuming that the confidentiality of responses remains protected – an issue we discuss in Steps 5 and 6 as well).

METHODS OF ADMINISTRATION AND DATA COLLECTION

Another decision to be made in the survey administration process is the primary method or type of administration desired. There are a host of different options depending on the needs and objectives of the survey effort. Fortunately, these choices are not mutually exclusive; practitioners will often employ more than one at a time (as in our example in Table 4.1). This range of administration methods can be described as varying along two primary dimensions: (a) the means of administration and (b) the means of data collection.

Regarding the method of administration, there are two options for the practitioner: distribute the instrument individually to respondents to complete on their own, or have them respond collectively in some form of orchestrated groups sessions. Individual methods are by far more popular in practice than collective assessments but, as with all choices in the survey process, each method has its strengths and weaknesses. Table 4.3 provides an overview of the basic differences in these two approaches. A review of Table 4.3 should make it evident as to why individual methods are preferred over collective ones. On-site survey administration tends to be a more expensive, complex and time-consuming process than individual methods. The on-site group-based survey sessions can have the benefit of (a) enhancing response rates by requiring individuals to

Table 4.3   Methods of survey administration

Individual	Collective
e.g. survey questionnaires mailed to employees' home addresses with return postage paid envelopes preprinted with an external collection source.	e.g. on-site survey 'capture sessions' offered three times a day across several weeks with independent proctors and secure data collection locked drop bags in a central location
• Greater privacy for respondent	• Less privacy for respondent
• Autonomy as to when/where to respond	• Fixed choices as to when/where to respond
• Individual choice to respond or not	• Individual can be required to attend session
• Response rates more affected by idiosyncrasies	• Response rates less affected by idiosyncrasies
• Responses less susceptible to intentional biases	• Responses more susceptible to intentional biases
• Fewer staff required to administer	• Staff intensive/costly to administer
• Responses returned via mail over time	• Responses collected immediately
• Highest level of confidentiality when used with outside source to collect data	• Potential for reduced levels of perceived confidentiality when collected on site

89

attend during working hours and (b) sending a good message regarding the level of commitment from management to the survey effort, but these positives can also backfire. For example, with an on-site administration method there is still no way to ensure that respondents feel secure about the confidentiality of their responses since they are being watched while they respond and, therefore, there is a greater potential for biases and response effects to occur. In addition, despite the positive corporate survey messages about taking time during business hours to complete the survey, individual managers do not always agree with this policy (since it is their people who are missing work, after all) and can sometimes sabotage this message completely. On the other hand, individual methods, regardless of the method of data collection (see discussion below), place a greater degree of trust in the respondent to complete and return the instrument on their own, which can sometimes lead to lower than desirable response rates in organizations where the importance of the survey effort has not been clearly communicated or established.

In those cases where an on-site plan is required, the logistics of the administration process must be clear and well defined to ensure an adequate level of response options for employees. Table 4.4 provides a sample schedule used for this type of on-site survey administration process. Note that in Table 4.4 the list of survey sessions was designed to provide optimal exposure at the same locations across different days and times. Even in this relatively simple example, the number of permutations is not insignificant. In addition to these variables, another consideration here was the administrator or survey proctor who was assigned to work at each of the settings. Since this person, too, can have an impact on the nature and quality of the data collected, varying the person across settings is also a consideration. In this way, it may be possible to examine the survey data for various effects or biases that may be attributable to the individual's instructions or mannerisms. Of course, one way to minimize the impact of

Table 4.4 Sample on-site survey administration plan

Location	Date	Time	Administrator
First Ave.	10-June	9.00–10.00 a.m.	1
Second Ave.	10-June	11.30–12.30 p.m.	2
Third Ave.	10-June	2.00–3.00 p.m.	3
Second Ave.	11-June	9.00–10.00 a.m.	1
Third Ave.	11-June	11.30–12.30 p.m.	2
First Ave.	11-June	2.00–3.00 p.m.	3
Third Ave.	12-June	9.00–10.00 a.m.	1
First Ave.	12-June	11.30–12.30 p.m.	2
Second Ave.	12-June	2.00–3.00 p.m.	3

individual differences is to have a clear and consistent script for the on-site survey administrator. Table 4.5 provides a sample script of this type.

The script in Table 4.5 covers many of the key issues required of the survey communication process discussed in Step 3, including the purpose and objectives of the survey, some background and context regarding the larger change effort of which it is a part, the specific format of the items and response forms included, how the confidentiality of the data is to be handled and who is going to have access to the individual responses. When the survey instrument is to be administered on site to people, it is often better to deal with these issues directly through the proctor than to use a more formal letter as would be the case in an individual method.

Besides the method of administration, the remaining key decision for survey administration concerns the type or method of data collection. Even when you have a well-defined and valid survey questionnaire in hand, there is still the issue of how to give it to people and by what means you intend to gather their responses. As with most aspects of the organizational survey process, once again there are several options, most of which can and often are used in conjunction with one another to meet various needs in the total administration process. Some of these methods include standard paper and pencil responses (e.g., circle or

Table 4.5 Survey administration script

[Total time for introduction: 15 minutes]

'Hello, my name is [Sir Vey Proctor] and I am here to talk you through the 1998 XYZ employee opinion survey process.

[*for ABC Consulting representatives*] . . .

'I am a representative from ABC Consulting Inc., an independent organization consulting firm in New York. We at ABC have developed the 1998 employee opinion survey you are about to complete.

[*all read as follows*] . . .

'Staff at ABC have been working with XYZ on a variety of projects over the past year. We have been involved in a merger and acquisition, and the development of this new employee survey. ABC has considerable experience with conducting large-scale organizational surveys with many different types and sizes of organizations.

'I am here specifically to help ensure that: (1) the survey process will be properly explained and consistently administered across the various departments and branches of the [bank], (2) that there is an impartial person to answer questions and concerns you may have, and (3) to collect the data immediately after you have completed the forms, and return them directly to ABC for processing.

'This is all part of a process to ensure the accuracy and confidentiality of the responses obtained. I cannot stress enough to you that your individual responses will not be revealed to anyone outside ABC. This survey is completely confidential. After scoring, your response form and write-in commentary sheet will be destroyed. Your responses will only be included in aggregate reports with other XYZ employees – never in isolation.

Table 4.5   continued

[Total time for introduction: 15 minutes]

'Let's now turn to the purpose of the survey itself. Why is the company conducting a culture survey at this time, and why are your responses important? A great deal of change has taken place in the organization over the last two years, including the merger and acquisitions, the new systems that have been put in place, structural changes, etc. and this can be unsettling and difficult to manage at times. Now that things have settled a bit and employees have been working together in new functions and relationships for a while, senior management is very interested in knowing how you feel about the organization. Thus, this survey has a large number of items covering many different aspects of XYZ including the pressures you face from your competitors, your awareness of the mission of the [bank], perceptions of senior and business unit leadership, how you feel about the computer systems, training and pay, the strengths and weakness of your managers, the helpfulness of the formal organizational structure, and your level of motivation and the overall performance of the [bank].

'There is a strong commitment from the top of XYZ to use the results to help people in their jobs and help the bank become a better place to work. To ensure the validity of our process going forward, it is important we get a strong initial baseline response. That means that our goal is to get *everyone* to participate. You are a very important part of the organization; your perceptions and observations are crucial to helping us understand what is good and what could be improved within the [bank] today. Thus, your participation is very important. While it is not required that you respond – this time is yours, we would strongly encourage you to take the time in the next hour to complete the survey.

'Can we get started?' [*If people do not wish to complete a survey, they can leave at this point.*]

'With the exception of the write-in comments included at the end, please answer all questions on the Response Form provided. On the Response Form, darken in, with a soft lead pencil, the circle representing your choice among the alternatives. The questionnaire form has a total of 125 questions for you to complete. Please do not write on the questionnaire booklets. Record all of your answers on the blue bubble form provided.

[*Distribute a booklet, 'bubble' answer sheet, and 'Write-in' Comments sheet to each person.*]

'Each question is rated on a five-point scale, with '1' and '5' reflecting the opposite ends of the scale. The sixth choice 'DK' (don't know) is only to be used if you feel you are unable to answer a particular item. Please consider the full range between 1 and 5 in making your response. Each statement should be answered according to your own experience and opinion, and should reflect your perception of present overall conditions. The second part of the answer sheet is the Write-in Comments sheet for any additional comments you may have – issues we didn't get to in the survey or you would like to expand on. As with the other results, these comments will be kept confidential by having them transcribed and grouped with others according to common themes as a part of the survey results analysis. Your comments will not be linked to you personally in any way.

'If you have any questions regarding the survey please let me know and I will come over and talk to you individually. If you have any questions in the future, please call ABC at [telephone number].'

tick an item on the survey document), optical scan forms wherein the appropriate bubble corresponding to an item in a survey booklet is darkened with pen or pencil, voice-response technology where people call into a central computer and enter their responses using the number pad on their telephones, on-line survey response forms either using an internal network or external web site, and even disk-based methods where the entire instrument is on a self-contained program run from a floppy disk and then returned. Table 4.6 provides a listing of these different data collection types and the pros and cons associated with their respective use. The more recent alternatives – i.e., options 3 to 5 – are very novel, exciting and therefore enticing to some practitioners, particularly those who are either enamoured with computer technology or who are bored with the more tried and tested traditional methods; however, pencil and paper and optical scan methods remain the most commonly used method of data collection in organizations today, for many of the reasons noted in Table 4.6.

On-line technology is making some very exciting inroads into the data collection process (Kuhnert and McCauley, 1996), but there are still some significant concerns and barriers to the full-scale use of these methods. We came across one of these quite recently. In this survey effort, conducted in a technological organization, after previously agreeing on, planning for and designing a custom paper survey based on optical scan response technology, the client decided at the last minute (in consultation with another key internal constituent group) that it would be more progressive and appropriate for the organization to use on-line response methodology instead as the primary means of collecting the survey data. It was his intention to provide all employees with a hard copy of the survey (and therefore not reducing the printing or distribution cost at all), and to have them link to an internal site to actually input their responses on-line. Of course, when he approached his own internal information technology people about designing such a system, he was informed that it would take at least an additional five weeks to design and make ready such a system, based on the already finalized instrument. Since timing was not a main concern in this project, the administration was held until the new system was ready. Unless practitioners have a fully functioning on-line system already in hand or purchase a shell (or template) from an external source, there are likely to be significant issues of implementation in this type of approach.

Security is a particular problem as well. Regarding the use of on-line survey systems, for example, if it is currently too unsafe for people to send their credit card information over a network (whether internal or external), then it is too insecure to protect people's sense of confidentiality in their survey data. Since e-mail leaves a trace from the respondent (unless it has been processed first through some sort of anonymizing processor), the source of the data point can always be determined. Placing controls on these systems does not always help the situation either. For example, the use of anonymous on-line methods as well as those based on voice response that do not have checks to identify users (for fear of intimidating people with respect to confidentiality), makes it much easier for people to abuse the systems by responding several times to the survey effort.

93

Table 4.6   Methods of survey data collection

	Positives	Negatives
1. Paper and pencil response	• Most intuitive survey approach to data collection • Allows great flexibility regarding types of items and scales • Participants work on the survey document • Moderate level of confidentiality (concerns regarding hand writing can be an issue) • Easy to change at last minute	• Costly to print large booklets • Costly to administer them via mail • Response burden can be high in long documents • Data processing is costly, complex, time-consuming and more prone to errors due to hand entry or scanning process • May require good writing skills
2. Optical scan response	• All data contained on single page • Easily faxed, low cost to mail • Ease and speed of data processing • Extremely low error rate • High level of confidentiality when individual completes in own time and mails themselves • Low-cost data entry	• Response burden higher when using optical scan form • Reduced flexibility in working with multiple types of items and scales on same form • Costly to change at last minute • Printing time can take weeks • Test-like appearance
3. Voice response/ telephone	• Data processing is immediate • Enhanced error correction at entry • Greater flexibility in use of context sensitive items and responses options • May be perceived as more interactive by respondents	• Often requires hard copy of survey to be printed and administered anyway • Reduced flexibility regarding length • Comments must be voice recorded • Confidentiality may be suspect • Costly to change at last minute • Potential for multiple responses from single individual unless tracked • Requires significant time for initial set-up
4. On-line response	• Data processing is immediate • Enhanced error correction at entry • Easy to administer on network • Easy to change at last minute	• Requires computer literacy • Requires network access/familiarity • Confidentiality highly suspect due to nature of IDs • Potential for multiple responses from single individual unless tracked • Requires significant time for initial set-up
5. Disk response	• Allows great flexibility regarding types of items and scales • Participants work on their own disk • Moderate level of confidentiality • Enhanced error correction at entry	• Requires computer literacy • Costly to produce disks and administer them through the mail • Greater levels of complexity and time in data processing due to disk reading and copying process • Requires significant time for initial set-up • Costly to change at last minute

For example, a disgruntled employee could potentially call in and provide his or her ratings many different times without ever being identified. While this same individual could potentially fill out more than one copy of a survey questionnaire or optical scan form by hand, these situations are less likely to occur with more traditional methods because (a) each individual receives only one copy of the instrument in any given form and must therefore actively request more copies rather than simple calling or logging on a second time, and (b) the time and effort required to complete the questionnaire using these types of systems is often enough to prevent their use a second time.

Of course, system abuse is not the only concern, nor the only decision point in the choice of methodology employed. Cost, flexibility of response format, speed of system design, cultural differences and access issues are also important. The cost of using optical scan technology is relatively low with regard to postage and data entry (as compared with key punching or mailing disk versions of a survey); however, even when custom designed and printed, these forms can often make it difficult to accommodate a variety of scale types and lengths (see Table 4.7 for a sample image of an optical scan form). For example, if 10,000 forms have already been printed based on a five-item scale format, if the client or a key member (e.g., the CEO) in the organization decides at the last minute to go with a six- or seven-point option, it is impossible to use the existing forms. Similarly, if the survey form is initially designed to accommodate 60 items in total, and ten more late additions are provided by some important constituent group (e.g., union representatives) at the last minute, the existing forms can be rendered useless as well. A carefully designed and planned survey instrument as described in Step 2 should not suffer from these types of changes just prior to survey administration, but similar situations do occur and these can be costly and time-consuming with optical scan methods. On the other hand, optical scan technology is simple to use for most people, familiar to many though not all cultures, easily mailed and faxed to various locations, highly individual in nature, and easily checked for errors during processing.

There are no conclusive results regarding which data collection method is superior; however, we were involved in a comparative study of survey methods conducted during a sample organizational survey, which raised some interesting issues. Having conducted a prior survey using only optical scan technology, the primary client in charge of administering the survey effort, an organization development specialist, wanted to implement and strongly encourage an internally designed and managed voice-response option as well as a more standard paper and pencil method for their resurvey process. There were two reasons for the use of a dual data collection methodology: a perceived reduction in cost associated with the internally designed voice-response option over more traditional methods, and an issue of reach – i.e., not all employees had equal access

Table 4.7   Sample optical scan form

1.	①②③④⑤	21.	①②③④⑤	41.	①②③④⑤
2.	①②③④⑤	22.	①②③④⑤	42.	①②③④⑤
3.	①②③④⑤	23.	①②③④⑤	43.	①②③④⑤
4.	①②③④⑤	24.	①②③④⑤	44.	①②③④⑤
5.	①②③④⑤	25.	①②③④⑤	45.	①②③④⑤
6.	①②③④⑤	26.	①②③④⑤	46.	①②③④⑤
7.	①②③④⑤	27.	①②③④⑤	47.	①②③④⑤
8.	①②③④⑤	28.	①②③④⑤	48.	①②③④⑤
9.	①②③④⑤	29.	①②③④⑤	49.	①②③④⑤
10.	①②③④⑤	30.	①②③④⑤	50.	①②③④⑤
11.	①②③④⑤	31.	①②③④⑤	51.	①②③④⑤
12.	①②③④⑤	32.	①②③④⑤	52.	①②③④⑤
13.	①②③④⑤	33.	①②③④⑤	53.	①②③④⑤
14.	①②③④⑤	34.	①②③④⑤	54.	①②③④⑤
15.	①②③④⑤	35.	①②③④⑤	55.	①②③④⑤
16.	①②③④⑤	36.	①②③④⑤	56.	①②③④⑤
17.	①②③④⑤	37.	①②③④⑤	57.	①②③④⑤
18.	①②③④⑤	38.	①②③④⑤	58.	①②③④⑤
19.	①②③④⑤	39.	①②③④⑤	59.	①②③④⑤
20.	①②③④⑤	40.	①②③④⑤	60.	①②③④⑤

to telephones (and definitely not to computer systems) but they could all receive mail. After some initial discussions relating to the information provided above, the survey administration plan involved multiple translations of the survey document and subsequent mailing of hard copies of the survey to a stratified random sample of 19,000 employees (representative of the total 54,000 employees in this global pharmaceuticals corporation). In addition to the mailout, a toll-free voice-response unit was established and widely promoted in each country and even across different regions to handle incoming calls from employees with a response protocol to screen inaccurate data as it was entered. All employees included in the sample received their copies of the survey instrument by mail; however, they were all given the choice of completing the survey on the document and returning it or calling in their responses using the voice-response units. Despite some significant problems with last minute changes to the voice-response protocol and issues inherent in setting up toll-free lines in different countries, the process was eventually launched using both methods. After a two-month response period, the survey effort closed with 70 per cent total rate of return – which is good, particularly in a large-scale global organization of this nature. Interestingly, and to the client's total surprise, among the approximately 13,000 responses, 65 per cent of employees chose to return the completed paper and pencil survey and only 35 per cent availed themselves of the voice-response technology. Thus, the anticipated cost savings associated with the use of the voice-response technology was not fully realized. Besides some of the difficulties already mentioned with the initial set-up of this system, data gathering errors were also introduced in the form of repeated responses due to a programming glitch. Some subsequent analyses of the full data collected from these two methods suggested that the employees using the voice-response option were in fact more *negative* in their perceptions (based on the ratings provided) than those responding via the paper and pencil survey questionnaire form. More specifically, when averaged across all 60 items in the survey, the mean rating (on a five-point scale) from the 8,700 people using paper and pencil methods was 3.36, compared with a mean of 3.24 for the 4,800 people choosing to use the voice-response option. Although not an enormous difference on an individual level, this is a very large and statistically significant effect for such a large number of respondents. This trend was also mirrored across about 60 per cent of the specific survey questions themselves including ratings of leadership, customer service and innovation.

RESPONSE RATES

In the organizational survey effort described above, the final response rate obtained was approximately 70 per cent of the sample used, which we said was good for a survey of this type. The response rate, of course, is calculated by taking the number of completed *usable survey responses* divided by the total number of survey instruments distributed (minus any that were undeliverable due to bad addresses or individuals no longer working in the organization). A response rate can range theoretically from 0 to 100 per cent, but in practice the practitioner can expect to achieve a response rate somewhere between 30 and 85 per cent. Some large corporations with well-established internal survey efforts regularly report response rates of 80 per cent or better (Kraut, 1996b), for example IBM, where the corporately sponsored opinion survey has been operating consistently for years; however, our experience with newly developed or revamped survey efforts across a variety of organizational settings

Table 4.8 Survey response rates experienced across various organizational settings

Industry type	Context of survey	Target population	Response rate (%)
Chemicals	Culture diagnosis and change	Employee sample	78
Communications	Change in strategic direction	Employee sample	53
Financial services	Change in strategic direction	Employee sample	41
Financial services	Cultural impact of mergers and acquisitions	Employee census	79
Financial services	Change in strategic direction	Employee census	37
High technology	Culture diagnosis and change	Employee sample	70
Information technology	Culture diagnosis and change	Employee census	58
Pharmaceuticals	Culture change following merger	Management census	73
Pharmaceuticals	Change in strategic direction	Employee census	57

has suggested considerably lower response rates (see Table 4.8 for a sampling of these).

Most survey professionals agree (e.g., Babbie, 1973; Edwards, et al., 1997; Rea and Parker, 1992) that a response rate of 50 per cent or better is adequate for analysis purposes, particularly when using an individual method of administration. Similarly, response rates above 65 or 70 per cent are considered good by most standards. The incremental value of a response rate of an additional ten percentage points higher than this is far less than the relative degree of concern for a survey response with ten percentage points below 50 per cent. In fact, anything below 50 per cent, particularly if a sample instead of a census was employed, is suspect regarding the appropriate levels of representation of employees (Kraut, 1996b). Survey response rates lower than 50 per cent can be common in organizational settings due to such issues as a resistive organizational culture, and/or poor administration methods, project planning, survey construction, communication, survey leadership and survey sponsorship. The use of monetary incentives included with the initial administration has been shown in a meta-analyses across many different studies (e.g., Church, 1993) to have a positive impact on response rates in mail surveys, but survey efforts in organizational settings do not usually have the financial resources required to follow this recommendation.

Where a response rate does fall below 50 per cent, one approach that can be used to examine the validity and representativeness of the data is to conduct a direct comparison of the demographic in the sample or total population surveyed versus those obtained in the survey. If the patterns of respondents are similar with respect to such variables as grade, age, gender, ethnicity, tenure in the organization, etc., there is some evidence to suggest that the responses may not be overly skewed to one specific group versus another effort (e.g., Burke,

Coruzzi and Church, 1996). This practice is equally well suited, and indeed recommended, for surveys with greater than 50 per cent response rates as well.

LEARNING WHILE DOING

The final point to be made regarding the survey administration process is a simple one, but important none the less. Much as we would like to think of survey efforts as discrete projects with a beginning and an end – particularly from the point of view of having a specific launch date and a closing date for returns – a survey is more appropriately thought of as a continuous process. As we stated earlier, it is advisable during an organizational survey effort to be prepared for various contingencies, setbacks and last-minute changes, and to have an administrative design that is as adaptable and flexible as possible.

CHECKLIST FOR STEP 4

1. Consider the implications of timing.
   Remember that the goal here is to obtain the best quantity and quality of responses with a clear set of objectives. These are key timing factors to consider:
   - What will be the impact on other organizational initiatives?
   - Are people already 'surveyed-out'?
   - How will a survey be received – i.e., positively or negatively?

2. Determine a project plan.
   - When will the survey be launched and when will it be closed?
   - The method by which the survey instrument is to be completed.
   - The respondents to whom the instruments are being distributed.
   - The means by which the instruments are going to be distributed.
   - The length of time respondents will have to complete and return the instrument.
   - The timing and types of additional information regarding the survey.

3. Decide whom to survey – sample versus census.
   Key considerations here are cost and the complexity of the administration process.

- Samples are easier, cheaper and useful between larger census administrations.
- A census is better for large communication, organization development and change initiatives.

4. Determine methods of administration and data collection.
   - Consider the impact of method on response rates.

5 Interpreting results

Look to the essence of a thing, whether it be a point of doctrine, of practice, or of interpretation.

Marcus Aurelius Antoninus

The prospect of statistically analysing data obtained from potentially thousands of individual responses collected during a survey effort can be daunting for many people, at least at first. Most people are simply not used to working with so much raw information. Once the initial shock of the size and complexity of the dataset has been absorbed, however, the budding survey practitioner will find that the analysis and interpretation phase is really a process of (a) creating and (b) communicating a story regarding the current state of the organization (or whatever the focal topic of the survey initiative). This step is concerned with the first of these – i.e. 'what is going on and why', while Step 6 discusses the second – i.e., sharing the 'what' and 'why' with others. In addition to detailing the specific stages involved in the analysis process, this section also covers some broader issues related to survey interpretation such as how to balance client expectations with realities (and limitations) inherent in the data, the use of norms and benchmarking data, and how to use write-in comments to enrich the data.

Before exploring any dataset, remember the basic goal of your efforts during this phase – i.e., information reduction. Whereas the concentration during both the survey development and the administration stages has been on collecting more rather than less information, now it is time to compress the volumes of opinions, attitudes and perceptions into a single coherent picture for the client (or your own) organization. When you begin to interpret survey results you are engaging in a process of data synthesis with the intended outcome being an accurate and meaningful distillation of a few main themes, trends and issues as reflected in the larger set of responses (see Figure 5.1).

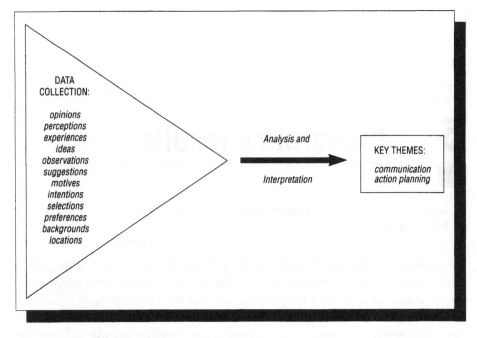

Figure 5.1 The distillation process

THE ROLE OF STATISTICS

Survey interpretation often involves the effective use of advanced statistical techniques – e.g. multiple regression, item response analysis, analysis of variance,
factor analysis, reliability analysis, and even structural equation modelling – but
these sophisticated tools are not *required* to produce an interesting and compelling set of findings. Like other types of tools, statistics are only helpful to
people who know how to use them and understand their strengths and weaknesses. Sometimes the uninformed use of statistics can go a long way to getting
the survey practitioner into trouble. For example, someone knows just enough to
ask the right questions but not enough to fully understand the complexities
inherent in the answers. We have been involved in a number of survey analysis
efforts (sometimes being called in just for this portion of the effort) during which
one of the client's recurring questions was 'tell me which findings are statistically significant'. This is, of course, a valid query. However, statistical significance is affected by four primary factors:

- the relative strength of the observed effect (i.e., difference between mean scores for a given pair of questions, or between averages across a series of items for two different regions or functions)
- the amount of variance obtained in the measures (i.e., the degree of similarity or disparity among individual responses to the same questions)
- the total size of the dataset (i.e., 100 employees versus 10,000 employees)
- the degree of precision or confidence required to state that a result is indeed statistically significant (e.g., 90 per cent confident, 95 per cent confident, 99 per cent confident, etc.),

therefore this question does not always result in a completely straightforward answer, which in turn, often confuses the client even more. To demonstrate this point, see Table 5.1 which is part of a letter provided in response to this very issue that we sent to one of our clients during a large staff survey effort.

These problems with the use of statistics can be compounded further in those cases where individuals with limited skill in this area attempt to use some type of statistical computer package to provide statistical results without fully understanding important assumptions and parameters involved in their use. These programs will always produce any number of pages of output, particularly when

Table 5.1 Response to question on statistical significance

In response to your request regarding significant differences among 93 and 94 survey data as well as within a single report (Directorate vs Department, item vs item, etc.), I have conducted a number of test analyses in order to provide you with the following rules of thumb. Please keep in mind that the information listed below is only a set of general recommendations for determining important and/or meaningful differences. Thus, in some cases, not all significant differences may be meaningful to consider (particularly if the sample sizes are very large), and not all non-significant differences may be unimportant.

Although the degree of variability among the different items does vary considerably, given the number of comparisons and the use of a similar scale (1–5) throughout most of the items, the primary consideration in determining a statistically significant difference among the survey results is the sample size (or number of respondents).

Sample Sizes for Each Comparison Group	Approximate Difference in Means Needed to Reach Statistical Significance
500 & above	.2
300–500	.3
150–300	.4
50–150	.5
20–50	.6

using the most recent group of programs that are fully menu driven and have interactive help screens regarding analysis commands. Good advice in this case is to use only programs and procedures with which one is very familiar. If more advanced analyses are desired or required, the survey practitioners should find someone with experience in survey analysis to assist in the process.

Keep in mind, however, that the knowledge and use of advanced research tools alone does not in and of itself guarantee a useful or actionable interpretation process either. As with most other things in life, survey analysis and interpretation requires a combination of both skill and experience in working with this type of information. There are many individuals in organizations, for example, with advanced research-related degrees but limited survey experience, who would probably be willing to run some complex set of analyses if asked. In many cases these same individuals will likely discover that it is much more difficult to create a complete story based on survey results than it is to simply run their favourite statistical procedures using a computer. This is one of the reasons, of course, why there are some external organizational consultants as well as some internal practitioners who specialize primarily in the conduct and interpretation of organizational survey efforts.

THE IMPORTANCE OF TIMING

Regardless of the level of expertise and statistical knowledge being brought to bear in this process, it is an unfortunate reality of most survey efforts, at least in our experience as well as that of others (e.g., Kraut, 1996b), that the analysis and interpretation stage is allotted the *shortest* amount of time in the total project plan. It might be desirable to have a two or three month period in which to conduct a comprehensive set of analyses and fully examine the data using all possible options, but this scenario is not usually an option. Most survey participants want to see the results as soon as possible and this results in pressure on the survey analysis team. Managers and employees seem to understand that it can take several months to develop the appropriate questions for use in the survey instrument itself; however, once they have completed their survey and dropped it in the mail the desire to see the results is almost immediate and tends to peak in just a few weeks (see Figure 5.2). Since people often complete their surveys at different times during an extended administration period, it can easily be a month between when the first and the last survey response forms are received. By the close of the administration process those people responding early are already eager to see the results and have been waiting several weeks. The energy created by participation in a survey effort can indeed be a positive force for organization development and change (e.g., Nadler, 1977), but it can

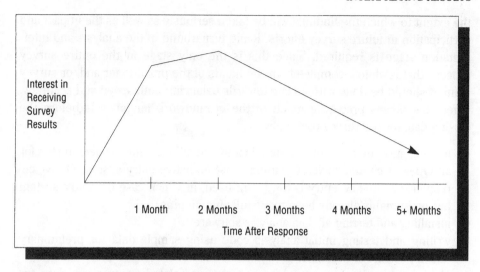

Figure 5.2   The relationship between response timing and level of interest in the results

also become a barrier when the feeling turns to one of either distrust or apathy regarding the outcome of the assessment process.

These effects translate to a need for the survey team to be able to work hard and fast during the analysis and interpretation stage. The time from final data collection to the first presentation of an overall report describing significant findings and trends to the survey sponsor and/or senior management is typically about two to three weeks from the close of the survey effort (in order to capitalize on as many returns as possible). Since there will likely be a lag in time between the initial delivery of the findings and the full-scale communication to all participants, except perhaps in very targeted survey applications (e.g., perceptions regarding a relatively small work group or function), keeping to this short time frame is necessary so that the results can be reported in a timely fashion to the larger organization.

In some instances the complexities of timing can be compounded, particularly when senior management are not pleased with the results obtained and have not readied themselves to accept criticism and acknowledge problem areas. In such cases, there is often a tendency to want to withhold the communication of the results to employees until after the message has been reworked and polished so that it better suits their particular objectives. Some level of hesitation and apprehension should probably always be expected when delivering the first set of survey findings to the sponsor and/or senior management, but if the data are held too long the results can become meaningless to employees damaging both

105

the extent to which the findings will be taken seriously as well as the impact and participation in future survey efforts. Rapid turnaround in the analysis and interpretation stage is required. Since this is the only stage in the entire survey process that is almost completely in the hands of the practitioner and/or survey team, it should be done with an eye towards balancing both speed and accuracy. Often this means preparing much of the groundwork for analysis before the closing date for the survey passes, by:

- making sure the data entry system is fully operational and has been tested for all types of contingencies (assuming that an active entry system like voice-response or on-line entry is not being used, in which case the entry system has presumably already been made fully functioning)
- installing and testing all data analysis software
- writing and testing initial analysis code using sample data (or preliminary data if possible or available)
- obtaining results from previous surveys or related comparison data for bench-marking purposes
- managing the clients' expectations and anxiety regarding issues with the collected data (e.g., ensuring confidentiality of individual responses, tallying the number of calls and queries into the process, providing updates on daily/weekly response rates, preparing clients for unexpected issues or problems that may arise in the data, etc.)
- preparing a comprehensive and thoughtful data analysis plan (e.g., familiarization with an overarching theoretical and/or conceptual model regarding potential relationships among variables or large sets of items, specifying additional relationships and/or trends to explore, targeting initial and final review dates for various elements of the analysis process, assigning roles and responsibilities for various tasks)
- developing a framework or outline of the final survey report. This is often based on the model used in the data collection process, and will help the analyst and the client prepare mentally and psychologically for the final product.

Having prepared the groundwork, the heart of the analysis process is now at hand. The remainder of this step provides an overview of the six main stages involved in the data analysis and interpretation process. Figure 5.3 provides a graphic representation of these stages in the form of an inverted triangle. Note that as one moves through each of the steps, the level of effort, time and complexity involved tends to increase. For the most part, this is because each stage requires greater levels of statistical processing and analysis capabilities. The process of analysing write-in comments, however, is the most time-consuming primarily because of the nature of working with individual responses (often

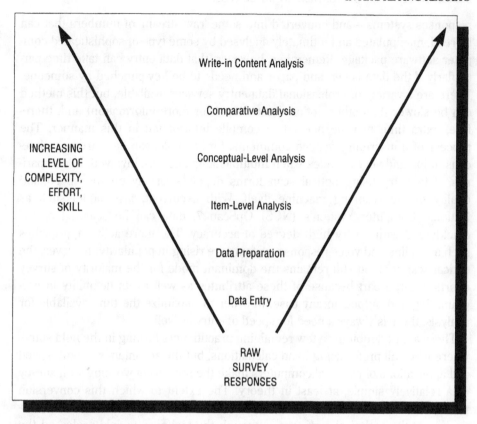

Figure 5.3   Six stages of survey analysis

voluminous in nature) as opposed to simple numerics. A detailed discussion of the relevant advanced statistical procedures related to survey analysis is not covered here, but pointers as to the utility of certain techniques and procedures as well as references for more information are provided during discussion of the various stages.

DATA ENTRY

The first stage for any sort of analysis or interpretation process requires that the survey responses be formally entered into some sort of database. Regardless of the method used for administration, the individual responses themselves must be converted from their natural state – whether it be optical scan forms, pen and paper survey questionnaires, voice-response data storage systems, or on-line

107

responses systems – and converted into some 'raw stream' of numbers that can be read, manipulated and ultimately analysed by some type of sophisticated computer software package. Remember, however, that data entry can take time particularly if the data is pen and paper and needs to be key-punched by someone. There are a variety of professional data entry services available, but this method can be slower than other options (see Step 4 for more information) and, therefore, extra time may be needed to compile information in this manner. The process of transcribing write-in comments, for example, can be extremely time-consuming and very complex when multiple languages are involved. In comparison, data entry using optical scan forms depends largely on the speed and quality of the scanning machine itself. With a current, fast model such as National Computer System's (NCS) OpScan 7, data can be scanned easily, quickly and with a very high degree of accuracy. The more active approaches such as on-line and voice-response systems are rising in popularity; however, the optical scan method still remains the dominant mode for the majority of survey efforts in large part because of these attributes as well as its flexibility in programming and output. In any case, in order to maximize the time available for analysis, there is always a need for speed of entry as well.

There are undoubtedly a few remaining practitioners lurking in the field somewhere who still prefer using hand calculations, but the advantages in both speed and applications of personal computers make the process of working with survey data relatively simple, at least in theory. The extent to which this conversion process proves difficult varies with both the method of collection and the sophistication of the technical staff (e.g., although the technical people professed the speed and utility of an on-line World Wide Web-based response system in one survey effort in which we were involved, when it came time to convert the data to numerical form for use in a database it took them two weeks to download the information in a usable form); however, there is almost always a way to extract the information in a manner that will be compatible with a variety of software packages.

A detailed discussion of the mechanics of these operations is beyond the scope of this section, suffice it to say that most systems can read and write one of two common options: (a) American Standard Code for Information Interchange (also known as ASCII or 'askey') text files where each response is represented by a continuous stream of numbers followed by a fixed return, or (b) comma delimited files (also known as CSV files) – a text file wherein each variable or question is separated by a comma in a long string of text. More sophisticated options include writing specific formats that are directly compatible with various popular database programs. Ensure that the individual managing the database system has a thorough understanding of the nature of the datastream being produced for analysis. The most important information for this process is:

108

1. The exact order or sequence in which individual responses to each question are listed including any demographics or background variables (e.g., years in the organization, age, location code, gender, department, response to survey question 1, question 2, question 3, etc.). In many cases, the order of variables used is a direct reflection of the order of the questions asked on the survey tool, but certain applications may require that items be listed in a variety of different sequences (e.g., when different sets of custom items are used for various functions or departments, or when the order has been varied for formatting or research reasons).

2. The number of records or lines of data per individual. Each line of data is followed by a hard return. In some cases and with some computer systems and applications, however, the number of columns needed to keep an entire individual set of responses on one line may exceed the number available. In these situations, multiple lines may be needed for each individual response.

3. The type of record format used to write the cases. There are two different options here. The first is called a fixed format in which the data contain exactly the same number of spaces for each variable or question regardless of whether or not there was a response obtained. With this type of datastream, it is easy to check that everything is in order with the raw scores because they will always end on the same last column (and have the same number of lines per response). The second option is called a variable format. In this format, the responses literally vary in length or the number spaces used are based on the pattern of responses obtained. Thus, if an individual answers only two questions on a survey of 100 items, there would still be only two spaces used in his or her datastream. This type of formatting system is particularly useful when responses to questions might vary in length, e.g. in a individual's name, occupational title or a detailed description of something. Note that in these types of files, some other type of indicator is required to separate responses to individual questions. Typical options used include a comma (as in the CSV file described above), a tab, or even a letter such as X or Z.

This information may seem somewhat simplistic, it is necessary none the less. If there are any errors or miscommunications regarding the above setup information, for example, it is almost a certainty that the analyses conducted will be entirely spurious and meaningless.

There are three basic types of software categories, and a host of specific products within each category, that are currently available to the practitioner with respect to the type of program that can be used for the data analysis and interpretation process. Table 5.2 provides an overview of the strengths and weaknesses

Table 5.2 Computer software options for analysis

Software category	Positives	Negatives	Sample product options
Statistical	Provides the latest and most advanced available statistical techniques	Difficult and complex to use with limited experience	Statistical Package for the Social Sciences (SPSS)
	Highly complex and flexible programming language	Will produce results even if it is not appropriate to do so More than is needed for basic analyses	Statistical Analysis System (SAS)
	Capable of working with extremely large files and numerous variables		BMDP LISREL
Database	Provides relational and multiple linkage among variables	Difficult and complex to use with limited experience	dBASE Microsoft Access
	Highly complex and flexible programming language	Often limited to only basic level of analysis for specific set of conditions	Paradox
	Works well with a variety for file formats and structures	More than is needed for basic analyses	Foxpro
Spreadsheet	Provides basic and easily understood functions for simple level analyses	Very limited analysis options	Lotus 1-2-3 Microsoft Excel
	Moderately complex and flexible in options	Some restraints regarding number of variables and/ or cases per worksheet	Quattro Pro
	Likely to have the widest range and flexibility regarding graphics and charts		

along with some sample applications for each type. The differences among these products were once considerable; however, in recent years the number and level of basic functions has begun to make them almost interchangeable for relatively simple and straightforward types of analyses. Almost all of these programs, for example, have the capability to produce excellent, high-quality reports and graphics in their most recent versions.

The choice of a program for use in this stage is dependent on a combination of (a) the range of functions and types of analyses available in the program, (b) the nature and complexity of the specific questions and investigations of interest, and (c) the familiarity, experience and skill level of the individual or survey team tasked with this process. The decision to use one or more of these programs should have been made before the data was ready to be input (see the comment on preparing the groundwork for analysis, above).

DATA PREPARATION

Some people think that once the raw survey data has been entered into a database system it means that it is automatically ready for analysis; in actuality, there is an important next stage that must be taken to prepare the data for subsequent exploration. That stage is called data preparation or data 'cleaning' because it represents the process of identifying and removing, or at least correcting, the various types of problematic responses that often occur in any data collection process. Many people who are only tangentially associated with survey efforts (including some of our clients in the past) are aware that this process occurs, none the less the raw data should be as clean and free of errors as possible before moving forward to the analysis and interpretation process. It is not uncommon, for example, for researchers and practitioners to find themselves in difficult situations midway through an analysis, or occasionally even later in the communication and roll-out process, only to find that blanks (also known as non-responses or missing cases) were being treated as real values in a set of computational averages (e.g. 9s – many programs use a 9 to represent blank responses) have been included so that the mean scores for various items have been artificially increased or skewed. Since these types of problems can affect the outcome of various analyses and therefore the nature of the survey story itself, the data must be examined and prepared thoroughly before proceeding with the next stage in the process. The survey items that are identified during the analysis phase as being the highest or most important to the organization, for example, should be due to actual perceptions or ratings made by respondents rather than because some chose *not* to answer the question and therefore skewed the results.

There are several different types of common problems or issues that need to be identified in the data preparation or cleaning process. Table 5.3 provides a listing of the main areas. Each of these problems will be discussed in greater detail later in this section, along with some suggested solutions. Although the identification of and ultimate solution to some of these concerns are relatively easy and straightforward, other issues are more subtle and may require considerable attention as well as some important decision-making on the part of the survey practitioner or team. However, the problems that are dealt with during this process are those due to individual respondents (e.g., not following directions) and not the instrument itself (e.g., badly constructed or unreliable items).

Table 5.3 Common problems/issues with survey data

Missing, incomplete or partially completed responses:
- blank optical scan form or questionnaire
- first five questions answered, the rest left blank.

Duplicate responses from same individual.

Problematic and/or intentional response patterns:
- all middle scores (e.g., 3s)
- all extreme scores (e.g., 1s or 5s)
- design scores (e.g., that make a graphic or range in clear sequences)
- responses to entire opscan form when the appropriate number is far less
- redundant/repeating scores (e.g., 1, 2, 3, 4, 5, 1, 2, 3, 4, 5, 1, 2, 3, 4, 5, etc.).

Incorrect use of scales:
- indicating a non-integer response on a scale with integers options (e.g., 2.5)
- selecting more than one response where only one is requested/needed.

Negatively worded items.

Inconsistencies in responses to similar items.

Damaged forms, computer malfunctions:
- optical scan forms that are torn, faxed or otherwise made unreadable to machines
- crashed disks, database systems that drop cases, glitches in writing cases.

In the former the solution usually lies with the individual datastream itself; in the latter, the solution is more systemic – i.e., it concerns modification of all responses for a given item or section.

MISSING, INCOMPLETE OR PARTIALLY COMPLETED RESPONSES

The first and most easily identifiable type of data problem that must be corrected is that of missing, incomplete or only partially completed responses to a survey instrument. It is an unfortunate fact that employees often return survey forms that have not been completed at all, or perhaps have only a few items with responses. Since blank returns can be accidentally counted towards the total response rates, or worse, included in various computational and analysis work as described in the example above, it is best to identify and remove them if necessary from the dataset. These types of forms or datastreams are easily seen in either hard copy form or on a database system. Once identified, if they are found to be completely blank they should be discarded and/or removed from the database. These forms can and should, of course, be counted as a blank return in the overall response rate but as a usable form. Partially completed responses, on the other hand, should be retained and used for analysis purposes unless the number of completed items is less than 10 per cent of the total set of questions provided (e.g., less than ten completed out of a total of 100 items on a survey). Less than 10 per cent complete suggests a significant problem with that respondent and raises questions about the validity of his or her data.

DUPLICATE RESPONSES FROM SAME INDIVIDUAL

Another potential problem in survey work, particularly when multiple forms of response options are provided such as a pen and paper survey and a voice-response unit, are duplicate responses. Some administration systems have built in safeguards to prevent this problem from occurring (e.g., providing individually coded questionnaires, key codes or response forms per each employee and not allowing unidentifiable responses to be used), but these are less common because they may suggest to some that the confidentiality of their individual responses may be compromised. Unless one of these types of systems is used, however, the dataset should be examined for duplicate responses as these can artificially alter the mean score and response rate obtained. It is quite possible (and has happened in one dataset we have seen), for example, that one disgruntled employee might try to have his or her responses entered into the system ten or more times, which is particularly relevant since his or her manager might be being rated on a specific section of the survey as well. A few duplications of this nature will probably not overly affect the survey findings but they can be unfairly damaging to the specific manager or department receiving feedback.

In practice, duplicate or multiple responses are relatively rare. Clients often ask that this issue be examined; however, it is usually only a very small number that appear to be duplicates. We have only seen significant cases of multiple responses in three or four organizations out of many surveyed. This is due, in large part, to the likelihood of receiving exactly the same set of responses being quite low in surveys with a large number of items. In fact, it is often uncommon to find exactly the same pattern of responses (whether they are duplicates or not) in large survey efforts. Finding such duplications in any dataset depends on (a) the number of questions asked and (b) the total quantity of responses obtained. Greater numbers of survey items on a questionnaire result in a reduced probability of finding exact matches that are not duplications, but larger databases with more people responding tends to offset this with greater probabilities of duplications. Based on probability theory, with 60 items or more and at least ten demographics, exact matches that are *not* duplications are highly unlikely regardless of the size of the dataset.

Identifying duplicate responses can be a difficult task, particularly in a large dataset with many items and/or many responses. The most efficient way to test for this problem is to use a sophisticated computer program to (a) sort the entire dataset in order of every single variable including the demographic responses, and then (b) using a 'lag function' test for an exact matching pattern of responses between each datastream and the next. When such a program is not available, the only other method is to sort the data using a basic word processing program and examine for duplicates by hand (not recommended). In those cases where an exact duplication is confirmed, however, and item number and sample size are large enough for this occurrence to be unlikely given probability theory, the duplication of or multiple responses should be deleted. Keep in mind, however, that one does not want to ever discard data with the same pattern of responses if they are in fact from different individuals, therefore careful examination of this issue is required.

PROBLEMATIC AND/OR INTENTIONAL RESPONSE PATTERNS

Another problem in survey work that is a more common occurrence is that of intentional response problems. Examples of these include such patterns as providing all middle or extreme scores on a survey – e.g., 3s, 1s or 5s on a five-point scale – or drawing patterns on a response form instead of actually responding. The latter is only possible with an optical scan form, the former occurs in all types of survey administration methods and is probably the most pervasive response problem short of return rates itself. Hostility, fear, apathy and anxiety are typically the causes of such problems. Since these data represent totally meaningless results at best, or totally biased ones (positively or negatively) at their worst, they need to be identified and removed before analyses and conclusions can be drawn with confidence.

In theory, the process of identification is simply a case of checking individual ratings for patterns that do not reflect actual opinions but some other type of response set. In practice, though, it is often much more difficult to spot these problems. It is relatively simple to notice responses with all the same scale option, but it is often much harder to find those with graphic patterns or ascending and descending patterns without looking through the individual questionnaires, optical scan forms or data strings themselves, which can be time-consuming. Therefore, many of these problems do actually get past the practitioner. With any luck, their impact in larger datasets should be relatively minimal.

Once identified, the datastream should definitely be removed. The problem, of course, is that in many cases the problematic pattern is not as clear cut as all responses using the same scale point. Instead, where the pattern may be questionable (e.g., mostly 3s, or 1s or 5s but not all), the decision is less clear and likely to be dependent on (a) total number of responses received and (b) similar types of ratings from others.

INCORRECT USE OF SCALES

A related issue to the one described above, but one that is less likely to reflect an intentional attempt at influencing the results, is that of incorrect use of the scales provided. Regardless of how many points are provided on a scale (e.g., 3, 5, 7, even 9) some respondents will decide to select a point not included as an option such as a 4.5 instead of a 4 or a 5. This problem is definitely worse with even rather than odd scales (see Step 2 for more detail on the difference between these options); however, the problem appears to be persistent regardless of the type of item. The other manifestation of incorrect use of scales is evident when people choose more than one response option such as 4 and 5 or both 'yes' and 'no' in response to a question. Both these examples are likely to occur more often in pen and paper or optical scan survey administration methods than in voice-response, disk-based or on-line systems, where the response choices are controlled through a computer.

If such a problem is present, the best option in both instances is to use an average (or the midpoint chosen as in the first example) of the total set of responses so that the data can be retained for analysis. Many data systems will not allow non-integer responses and/or the record formatting may result in a missing entry for these responses, thereby making this option unavailable. In such situations, the practitioner can try to merge these data points into the data-base at a later date or, more commonly, ensure that they are entered into the system as blanks. It is not always desirable to discard data that appear to be legit-imate; however, a scale was provided which should have been able to accurately capture the perceptions of the respondent. If everyone failed to respond appro-priately the item itself would be suspect and likely discarded completely, but with only a few midpoint responses it is better to assume that the respondent could not appropriately make a discrimination on the existing scale and, there-fore, their responses for those questions should be dropped (but not for that entire respondent). If the responses for a given item are truly categorical in nature (e.g., 'What is your primary work location?', or yes/no questions such as 'Do you have a personal computer at your desk?'), the data must be discarded if it does not fit the response options provided.

NEGATIVELY WORDED ITEMS

Another type of data problem concerns a specific type of question – i.e., those that have been negatively worded. Some survey professionals consider these to be useful for testing the awareness of the respondent and keeping them on their toes, other practitioners such as ourselves consider these types of items to have more problems than benefits (see Step 2). The issue here is that people often (a) fail to read these items carefully enough and therefore respond incorrectly, or (b) do not understand the negative wording itself. Presumably the latter concern has been corrected during a thorough testing process, but sometimes bad items do slip through. In any case, always check negatively worded items to ensure that individuals responded appropriately and accurately.

Often, the best way to check data is by comparing a mean score for the negatively worded item with a positively worded one with a similar content or theme. If the item did not produce ratings that parallel those of other items from the same individual or there are other types of abnormalities inherent in the response set, it probably should be dropped from analysis. If a negatively worded item is to be used for analysis purposes, responses should be recoded so that they match the direction of the other ratings in the survey. For example, if 1 was positive and 5 negative for a particular item, but most others on the survey had 5 as positive and 1 as negative, then the first item should be reverse scored. This way, the means will be more consistent when examined. The only caution here is that this recoding process should be carefully noted in reporting and/or communications using this item.

INCONSISTENCIES IN RESPONSES TO SIMILAR ITEMS

The final problem inherent in individual responses which is both difficult to identify and even more difficult to correct, but should be mentioned none the less, is the problem of inconsistency in responses. Often a result of inattention or occasional negativity towards the survey effort, two different items with the same general content can receive very divergent ratings. Conversely, a negatively worded item might not reflect the opposite of a positively worded one with a similar content focus as described above (see Table 5.4 for an example). These problems are often difficult to identify on an individual level without complex programming using a statistical or database computer program (reliability is a method for testing the general tendency across the entire dataset); however, they often remain in the database despite the interests of the practitioner.

DAMAGED FORMS, COMPUTER MALFUNCTIONS

The problems of damaged forms and computer malfunctions are common enough occurrences that often need to be dealt with in data preparation and cleaning procedures. With optical scan systems, for example, forms can become

Table 5.4   Consistency in responses

	Positive and negative questions	Responses
Consistent responses	a. To what extent is your manager effective at communicating with others?	5
	b. To what extent does your manager have difficulty communicating with others?	1
Inconsistent responses	a. To what extent is your manager effective at communicating with others?	5
	b. To what extent does your manager have difficulty communicating with others?	5

easily damaged and otherwise unreadable when torn, faxed or marked with pen instead of pencil (for those systems that read only pencil). These responses have to be either 're-bubbled' or entered into the data system by hand. In either case, there is a significant loss in both speed and accuracy for those individual responses. Similarly, frequent backups of active data collection methods such as voice-response units or on-line web site systems are highly recommended since there is no hard copy of the scores being obtained. Therefore a simple glitch in the computer's procedure could cause a permanent loss to the database.

ITEM-LEVEL ANALYSIS

Now that the data have been successfully cleaned and prepared the real part of the analysis and interpretation process can begin. As with most complex processes, there are several levels of analysis that one can progress through in examining survey data (see Figure 5.3). The first, most intuitive, and least statistically complex approach to data exploration is the item-level analysis. As the name suggests, at its most basic this is simply the process of examining the frequencies and descriptive statistics (e.g., means, standard deviations, ranges, and percentage of non-responses or don't knows) for each item on the survey across all responses obtained. Table 5.5 provides an overview of the information that can be obtained from each of these simple calculations. Since this type of information can easily be generated using almost any type of computer program including spreadsheets, statistical packages or databases, it is quite common among survey practitioners without advanced degrees or experience in research procedures for entire analyses to be conducted using only these core methods. Even if more advanced analyses are intended, the data should first be examined from this perspective.

117

Table 5.5 Descriptive statistics and the information provided

Descriptive Statistic	Information
Frequency	The relative number (and percentage) of people responding to each scale option for a given item. Most useful for demographic and categorical questions.
Mean	The average response obtained for a given item across all respondents. Most useful for Likert scale items (e.g., extent present, satisfaction, agree–disagree, etc.). Often used to identify the top 5 or 10 highest rated items (most positive), as well as the lowest 5 or 10 rated items (most negative).
Standard deviation	The degree to which ratings of a given item ranged across all respondents. Very useful in determining if item 'worked' or not across different sets of respondents. Also useful in determining the degree to which responses followed a normal distribution or were significantly skewed towards one end or another of the scale. Good indicator of whether or not the item will be helpful in more advanced analyses to determine complex relationships as well.
Range	The degree to which respondents rated the item using the full scale (i.e., all points provided) versus choosing middle range scores. Lack of full use of scale in large samples may suggest a problem with a particular item.
Percent non-response, not applicable or don't know	The relative number of people that did not or could not provide a response to a given item. Can be very useful as a data point itself (e.g., percentage don't know about how the formal performance appraisal process works), as well as important in identifying items that may be problematic or not well understood by respondents. Often items with high percentages on non-response are indicated as such on a formal report, and then dropped from more complex analyses.

There are two objectives or intended outcomes for this type of analysis pro-cedure. First, since the average responses to each of the survey questions are the primary source for all subsequent analyses and interpretation, identify items that did not work effectively or at all. Similar to the data preparation stage described above, the idea here is to identify any problematic items so that they can be corrected, put aside for the time being or, in extreme situations, removed from the database entirely. These are items which for one reason or another received significantly fewer responses in the form of don't knows or blanks than most others on the survey. However, these types of questions may still be useful and should be reported somewhere in the final presentation, but when 15 per cent or more of the responses were blank these should be interpreted with some caution and/or flagged for more detailed examination. Similarly, if responses to negatively worded items appear to be in opposition to the general trend on posi-tive questions with similar content, there may be a question as to their validity as

118

Table 5.6   Identifying response patterns

	1	2	3	4	5	Don't know
Q1. To what extent are promotions and assignments based on fair and objective assessment of people's skills?	3.2%	7.5%	37.5%	23.3%	8%	20.5%
Q2. To what extent do you feel adequately compensated for the work that you do?	25.1%	19.1%	32.0%	17.1%	6.6%	0.1%

well. Advanced statistics such as reliability analysis (i.e., do the items move together with each other in patterns) and item response theory analysis (i.e., do the items reach appropriate thresholds that suggest good response characteristics) are available, but the quickest and easiest tests are made using simpler measures. Frequencies are often the most useful here. In Table 5.6, for example, it is clear that while the full range of the scale was used on question 1, 20.5 per cent of respondents did not feel they could answer the question regarding the fairness of promotions given. Compare this with the responses obtained for question 2 regarding the perceived adequacy of the compensation plan. In this case, the non-response information on question 1 is actually usable and useful data since this suggests other possibilities.

Of course, in the results for this one item (question 1) alone, there are two entirely different possible interpretations that can be made, which in turn have very different recommendations for action associated with them. It could be, for example, that many respondents are simply unaware of the organizational processes and criteria used for promotion because they are not well communicated either by the Human Resources function or by their individual manager. On the other hand, it is also possible that this finding reflects a set of negative attitudes or experiences towards the formal promotion system. Or, to make matters more complex, perhaps the 20.5 per cent are all originating from only one or two departments or functions and are not a general trend across all respondents. This is a good example of the complexities inherent in the survey interpretation process, showing it to be an art as well as a science. There are never definitive answers to be obtained from survey responses (these require face-to-face conversations with employees); however, one of the best ways for a practitioner to determine which of these interpretations is more likely to be accurate is through examination of other related items with similar content, the use of advanced statistics to determine complex relationships among groups of

119

Table 5.7 Sample item sorting by mean score obtained

Item text	Mean	Ranking
1. To what extent does your manager stand up for what he/she believes?	4.21	1
2. To what extent does your manager take public responsibility for mistakes?	3.23	2
3. To what extent does your manager contribute actively and openly to the work of the team?	3.02	3
4. To what extent does your manager operate truthfully when delivering good or bad news?	2.07	4
5. To what extent does your manager deal with problems objectively and fairly?	1.99	5
6. To what extent does your manager take appropriate action about poor performance from his/her staff?	1.65	6

items, or through an analysis of the write-in comments provided (if these were collected).

The second objective in item-level analysis is to determine the highest and lowest rated items and to begin to look for emerging patterns or themes in the data. This involves a simple sorting and examination of all the relevant items on the survey from high to low. Some practitioners prefer to base their analysis work on categorical schemes such as 'percentage favourable' (i.e., the percentage responding to the top two scale points on a five-point scale such as 4 and 5), but the most complete method that uses all the data obtained is to use the average rating for each item. Once all the items have been sorted from highest to lowest, it is a relatively simple task to examine the top ten or twenty and the corresponding lowest ten or twenty items for (a) specific item ratings and (b) any general patterns that might be evident. Table 5.7 provides a sample listing of this type of analysis.

Keep in mind, however, that this process is a relative one – that is, it assumes that the highest and lowest rated scores obtained are indeed positive and negative findings respectively. While this is a workable assumption most of the time, it is not always the case. For example, if the five highest rated items on a survey using a five-point scale are all less than 3.10 the survey team would be hard pressed to claim that these responses as *positive aspects of the organization* since the mean scores are so close to the midpoint of the scale. Rather the interpretation would probably have to be something like employees in this organization are generally very unhappy or dissatisfied (or perhaps simply tough raters) and that these are the areas that received the highest ratings relative to other questions. Conversely, if the lowest ratings received on a survey again using the same five-point scale are all above 3.10 this would suggest that employees are somewhat pleased overall and that the problem areas are probably not important issues for most people. Once again although such patterns are uncommon, most large surveys using a five-point scale do yield mean results with some items above a 4.0 and some below a 2.0, these problem situations, while clearly not insurmountable, can and do occur making interpretation difficult. There is one caveat here, however, to this approach. If survey questions are to be examined in this manner it is imperative that two conditions be met:

1. All negatively worded items must be recoded to match the scales of the positively worded ones.
2. All items ranked together must use the same scales or, at the very least, scales with similar points to them.

Only compare items in this manner with like characteristics. There is no point, for example, in ranking means for items on a seven-point scale along with those using a three-point scale – it just does not make sense since the three–point items will always yield lower mean scores. Similarly, if a series of items have been rated using a unipolar extent scale such as 'the extent to which this behaviour is practised' it is probably not appropriate to rank these along with items rated using a bipolar agree–disagree scale, even if the number of points used in both scales is the same. In cases like these with significantly different scale lengths, points or related issues (e.g., ranked items, categorical responses) these questions should be examined independently of each other.

Besides the sorting process itself, there are a few rules of thumb that are helpful when evaluating item-level mean scores in a survey. First, don't expect the average of the entire survey to be the midpoint of the scale provided. Just because you use a five-point scale does not mean that the average should be about a 3, or a 5 with a nine-point scale. Most practitioners will concentrate on the highest and lowest items, but if a midpoint cut-off value is needed, the best method for determining one is to compute an overall average rating across all survey items (assuming similar scales as noted above). This value is then used to calibrate the midpoint and assess the degree to which various items are generally positive or negative. For the data presented in Table 5.5, for example, the total mean is 2.70. This indicates that any items falling below this can be considered anywhere from mildly to significantly negatively rated. Conversely, those above this rating are generally positive to very positive as far as the survey results themselves are concerned.

This calibration process will provide the most accurate method for assessing positive and negative values, a general rule of thumb based on survey experience is that all items that receive mean ratings above a 4.0 on a five-point scale or above a 6.0 when using a seven-point scale are generally very positive and strong findings. Similarly, most items with mean scores below a 2.0 or even a 2.5 at the low end regardless of the scale tend to represent significant problem areas. Whether or not any or all of these items become the focal points for the overall interpretation depends on other factors including the extent to which more complex conceptual models, frameworks or analysis are used to explore relationships.

CONCEPTUAL-LEVEL ANALYSIS

Once the survey practitioner and/or survey team has a thorough understanding of the descriptive statistics and item-level means, the next stage in the data interpretation process is a conceptual level analysis. Although this stage does not have to be overly complex nor does it require a working knowledge of advanced statistics, this is where the most advanced procedures and theoretical models are applied to provide a more complete and rich understanding of the relationships inherent in the survey data collected. This is what survey practitioners live for and where their expertise is best used. The goal is to use some type of overarching framework, model, theory, values, principles or even a set of observed relationships among variables that best 'fits' or describes what is going on in the results. The task is to generate four or five main areas or themes out of the entire survey dataset that can be used to explain or characterize the results and drive action planning. This is not always an easy or a simple task, but if done correctly it can make the survey results literally 'come alive' for the end client and the organization as a whole as well.

There are two basic approaches to conducting a conceptual level analysis: use an existing model or build one empirically from the data itself. Each of these approaches are described below.

Probably the most common application of a conceptual analysis is the use of an existing framework that is applied to the interpretation and perhaps even the analysis plan for the data. Often, this same model may have been used to guide the item development and construction process with respect to content areas to cover as well (see Step 2). In any case, the idea is to provide an overarching means of connecting different ideas and aspects of organizational life together in a comprehensive whole. It is for this reason, then, that in many instances, this guiding framework is provided by a well-developed, theoretically sound and widely used organizational model such as the Burke–Litwin model of organizational change and performance (Burke and Litwin, 1992), or the Nadler–Tushman congruence model (Nadler and Tushman, 1992). Those readers interested in learning more about either of these two models or other related approaches to diagnostic work in organization development and change efforts should see Burke (1994) for a good summary of this area. However, it matters less which particular perspective is chosen, as long as it provides enough latitude in its categories, descriptions or proposed relationships among variables to be relevant to the issues at hand.

It is for this reason, for example, that many survey efforts are designed and interpreted not around a theoretical model but instead with regard to some set of important values, principles or concepts that are specific to the organization itself. Once again, as we have mentioned several times before in earlier chapters, it is important to link the survey objectives, content and interpretation to relevant, important and visible elements of the organization such as the mission statement, core competencies or components of a new vision statement. This is one of the means by which survey results are given significance and therefore make an impact. Such was the case at SmithKline Beecham (Burke and Jackson, 1991) for example, where an organizational survey effort was used during the initial stages of the merger to (a) assess main issues that needed to be dealt with during the coming years in the management of the merger process, and (b) simultaneously communicate the new desired culture and leadership practices deemed important for the future success of the organization. The Burke–Litwin model was used as a driving force behind the design and interpretation of the survey tool (e.g., Burke and Jackson, 1991), but in the end the results were reframed and communicated to employees using the new five core values and nine leadership principles. The use of more than one model or framework is not always easy to reconcile when examining the raw data and creating a story; however, it is not uncommon when working with different professional groups and practitioners, particularly since most external survey consultants already have their own models well in hand.

When working with any type of pre-existing model or framework the standard and most basic approach is to use the primary variables, factors or content areas provided in the model (e.g., senior leadership, information systems, culture, motivation, reward systems) to classify and subsequently create averages or summary scores for each area. Questions reflecting various aspects of communication such as clarity, speed and consistency of messages received might be placed in a category reflecting corporate communication systems. This way, the information contained in the multitude of individual items can be condensed into a series of eight to twelve main categories that are all theoretically and conceptually similar in content. Figure 5.4 provides a sample of this type of conceptual analysis based on a comparison of summary scores. This type of conceptual approach – i.e., generating averages – is well within the means of a basic computer program; however, the added benefit of more advanced packages and statistics here is the notion that each item belongs in the category selected can be empirically tested using procedures such as reliability analysis, confirmatory

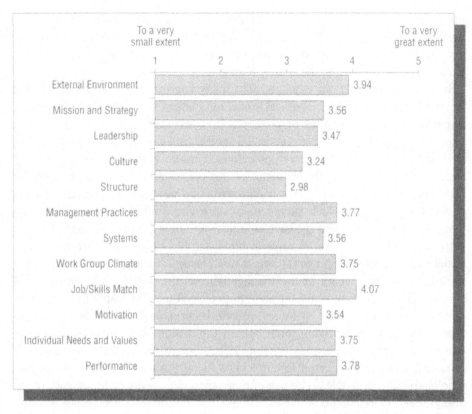

Figure 5.4 Sample conceptual-level analysis using summary scores derived from the Burke-Litwin model

factor analysis, multiple regressions and even structural equation modelling. Regardless of whether the item was categorized at the design and construction stage before the survey was administered or after the data have all been collected and examined at the individual item level, these types of statistical procedures can help better place individual items within main categories. Of course, if the conceptual analysis does not go beyond the categorization scheme, and the content averages such as those listed in Figure 5.4 are not used for decision-making purposes, it matters less whether or not the item truly belongs in a given category. In those cases where content areas such as these are important or truly meaningful, as in our use for example of the Burke–Litwin model for guiding diagnosis and organizational change initiatives, it is very important that the items be tested and moved or deleted if necessary so that model best fits the data at hand before proceeding further.

For those interested in going even further with this type of approach, the next logical application of a conceptual model is to test for relationships among the larger variables or categories described using inferential statistics. While this can only truly be done using advanced statistical modelling techniques such as multiple regression or structural equation modelling (there is no simple substitute other than, perhaps, simple correlations which are often difficult to interpret), the results of this type of advanced analysis are often worth the extra effort and can be very insightful into the underlying dynamics of a dataset. Without going into too much detail here, this process involves an analysis of the relationships among the variables described in the conceptual model or categorizing framework being used. By examining which types of variables are covaried with (or related to) others, a link can be drawn between changes or movements in one area and corresponding changes or movements in another. For those interested in more information regarding multivariate statistics in general see Pedhauzer (1982) and Tabachnick and Fidell (1989). More specific information regarding the use of these methods in survey analysis can be found in Babbie (1973), Berk (1983), Schumacker and Lomax (1996) and Stolzenberg and Land (1982).

Figure 5.5 provides an example of what the outcome of this type of more inferential approach might look like when using the same framework as in Figure 5.4. Based on an examination of these results (and with some knowledge of the organization being surveyed), it was apparent that performance in this financial services organization was being driven primarily by a combination of employees' understanding and awareness of the newly articulated mission and strategy, the rigidity inherent in the existing culture, the degree to which the day-to-day climate was generally positive or negative regarding the change effort and the specific behaviours exhibited by middle management in support of the change effort. Based on these findings and the strength of the relationships observed, some of the initiatives proposed included (a) enhancing and clarifying communications regarding the mission and strategy, and (b) multirater feedback aimed at middle managers in order to change their immediate behaviours, positively enhance the climate experienced by employees and, over time, impact the culture of the organization itself.

However, a word or two of caution should be noted regarding the use of these types of advanced modelling procedures. The results produced from this type of survey analysis do present a strong picture of the problems and potential solutions in the organization, but it also has the potential to cloud or obscure the more straightforward findings that are typically obtained. For example, there may be significant problem areas in a survey where people consistently provide low ratings and are clearly unhappy in their jobs, but that do not appear in this type of analysis because responses do not covary or move with other items. If everyone in the organization is in complete agreement that the management information systems are antiquated and lacking in speed and facility, that finding

125

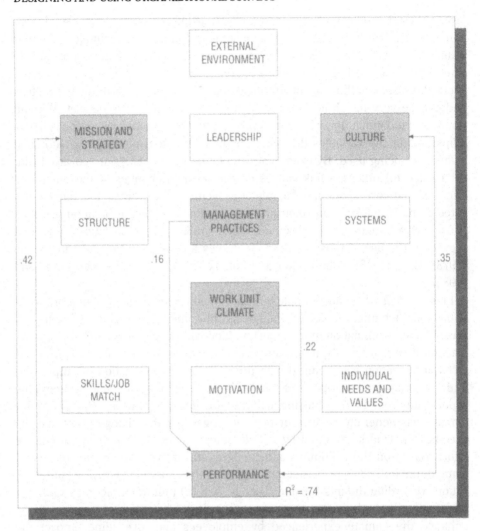

Figure 5.5 Sample conceptual-level analysis using advanced modelling techniques
Adapted with permission from W. Burke et al. *Organizational Surveys: Tools for Assessment and Change* © 1996 Jossey-Bass Inc., Publishers. All rights reserved.

is likely to be missed if a modelling analysis is the primary means of the interpretation and subsequent action planning process (since this variable will not be likely to covary with any others). This is one of the main reasons why the standard item level analysis approach is always recommended as the first step in any analysis plan – i.e., so that the survey team has a solid understanding first of the basic highs and lows from the individual ratings themselves before moving on to more complex exploration.

Besides the use of existing models or frameworks, the other main option for a level conceptual survey analysis, albeit less often employed, is to generate a new model based on the relationships inherent in the dataset at hand. The survey responses themselves are examined using a number of different sophisticated statistical techniques (e.g., factor analyses and structural equation modelling) in order to create a conceptual framework or set of interrelated categories that best describe the data obtained. While some practitioners, and particularly more traditionally oriented researchers, would argue that this type of approach is fundamentally flawed due to its tautological nature (arguing instead for a theoretically derived framework), in some situations this approach can be very useful. Occasionally, for example, the data as analysed according to an existing framework may not make enough of a compelling story to motivate people to action. In other situations, it may be that certain individuals would rather use the data itself (rather than a formal model) as the motivating factor. In fact, for those organizations with senior leaders who refuse to accept the notion that any pre-existing model or theory can represent the issues in their organization, creating a new framework is often one of the few safe alternatives to chaos and ultimate rejection of the survey results.

There are other situations when this approach may be useful in conjunction with an analysis plan driven by an existing conceptual model or framework as well. Let us say you have conducted a survey with a series of items representing each of the 12 boxes or variables corresponding to the Burke–Litwin model described above. Now, in looking at the results you realize that while you do have a clearly defined conceptual set of items in the management practices category (i.e., ratings of specific behaviours of middle managers by their subordinates), there are over 25 different behaviours that comprise this content area making a general interpretation of management practices somewhat difficult. You could conduct a basic item-level analysis by simply sorting the items in this section from most to least practised, a more empirical approach would be to use a principle components factor analysis procedure to isolate four or five specific groupings of items that hang or covary together statistically. In this application, the content of the items themselves will drive what these categories or factors are called. These factors could then be used to create management practices summary scores that are likely to make further interpretation and feedback more useful to others who have actually to work with these results. For most people, it is much easier to grasp only a few concepts, such as communication style, rewarding and recognizing others, personifying leadership, managing the task and empowering others than it is to work through a list of 25 individual items and associated responses. And remember, these data are for only one section out of possibly 12 on the survey so it is important that it be examined and presented in a way that people can understand and ultimately use for positive change.

127

COMPARATIVE ANALYSIS

An entirely different set of techniques that are applicable and commonly used in large-scale survey work are comparative analyses. Simply put, these approaches are directed primarily at understanding a specific set of results from a survey effort in comparison to some other similar type of information collected either at the same time, or a different time, or even within a different organization. The information and subsequently the interpretations and recommendations obtained from these types of investigations are considerably divergent in focus from the types described in the analysis options above. Rather than specifying general relationships or patterns in the data as in the conceptual analysis, they are more likely to point to significant differences in perceptions among specific groups (e.g., US employees versus UK employees in a multinational corporation), across extended time frames (e.g., time 1 versus time 2) or across different organizations and industries (e.g., external bench-marking of best practices). These three examples represent quite well the three general types of comparative analyses that can be performed on survey data. Each of these is described in more detail below.

The first and most intuitive form of comparative analysis is one which examines differences in survey ratings (using either items, conceptual variables and summary scores or even a total average survey response) by various groups, functions, areas, experiences, demographic information, or other categorizing variables used to clearly differentiate among types of people. For want of a better term, we have labelled these *comparisons by type*. The primary statistics used in these cases tend to be analyses of variance (ANOVA) because they focus on group differences. The most common sets of comparative analysis of this type are done by background characteristics such as tenure, education, gender or ethnicity to look for significant trends in responses. Other useful options might include questions that assess the respondent's participation or experience with a particular event such as a performance appraisal, various training courses, or even a prior survey effort. Table 5.8 provides some sample variables of this type and the corresponding types of interesting questions that might be answered with such an analysis.

A word of caution here as well. While the results obtained from these types of analyses can provide important information for interpretation and action planning purposes, the survey practitioner should not go too far with these comparative tests. In most cases there are likely to be far more variables available for comparative investigations than are practical given the need for a timely and concise analysis and interpretation of the results. Remember that the idea of engaging in the data analysis process in the first place is to condense the information collected into main trends and relationships, and not to expand the

Table 5.8 Comparative analyses using demographic variables

Variable	Question or information of interest
Location	Are there major differences among respondents from different regions or countries?
Age	Do younger employees feel differently about the company or their jobs than older ones?
Tenure	Do employees who have been with the company longer have more positive or negative attitudes?
Ethnicity	Do different groups experience the same level of treatment from managers?
Training	Do employees who have taken various training classes rate their knowledge of their jobs higher or have higher morale?
Gender	Do males and females differ in their perceptions of the fairness of reward and recognition policies?
Level	Do senior managers have different perceptions about the strengths and weaknesses of the organization than do middle managers or shop-floor service providers?

amount of information provided. However, some practitioners have a tendency to err on the side of 'information overload' by providing numerous iterations of variables cut by demographics and other categories to the point that the core messages in the data are lost to the end-user – i.e., the client or survey sponsor. While this type of detail is extremely important in the action planning stages (more on how this is generated and used in Steps 6 and 7), it can be very cumbersome and ineffectual to provide too much information of this type too early in the process. In most cases, the only comparative results that should be retained and explored in detail at the analysis level are those that truly *reflect main issues* that need to be recognized and considered at the survey sponsor (typically corporate) level. In a merger of two organizations, for example, differences between employees from the two former organizations might be of extreme importance and relevance, particularly if there are significant and powerful differences in perceptions. It probably makes less sense to include this type of information, however, in an interpretation where there are few differences evident or this issue is of less relevance. Results such as these can be, and often are, added as an appendix to a formal report later in the process.

The second type of comparative analysis is achieved using additional data external to the current survey effort itself – i.e., *comparisons over time*. Often, the burning question here is have perceptions improved since last year? Most organizations that have an institutionalized survey process, for example IBM or others in the Mayflower consortium (Johnson, 1996), generate time-based comparative analyses as part of the standard analysis procedure to look for trends in general attitudes and perceptions of employees. With these types of survey

129

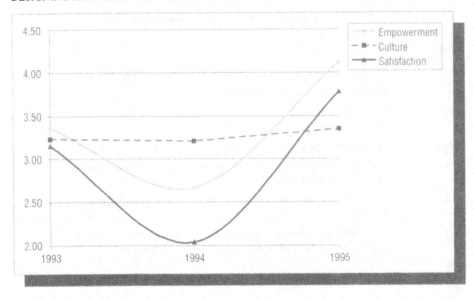

Figure 5.6   Sample comparative analysis using ratings over time

systems, senior management, HR and/or the organization development function can see quite easily if the changes made in-between assessments yielded a positive or negative effect on employees' ratings. This is one of the reasons why organizations undergoing significant change efforts in their mission, vision, values or structure, for example, implement an organizational survey effort to measure the impact and success of the change process over time (e.g., Burke, Coruzzi and Church, 1996; Waclawski, 1996b).

Figure 5.6 provides a good example of how one of these analyses might be used to explore changes in main content-related areas during the introduction and internalization of new empowerment-related management practices. For this example, let us assume that these new practices were intended to have a significant impact on the extent to which employees felt empowered in their jobs as well as the extent to which the organizational culture was supportive of innovation in the workplace. In examining the data, it is clear from this analysis, even though only three conceptual variables are being used, that (a) perceptions of empowerment and employee satisfaction seem to be highly related, and (b) while these were negative during the time when the new practices were first introduced (1994), employees appear to be feeling much more positive about both aspects in 1995 at which time the new concepts have taken hold. In comparison it is interesting that the culture of the organization does not seem to have been affected one way or the other during this change process. Ratings in this area were surprisingly stable over the course of two years. Since significant changes in organizational culture often take more than a year or two, however, this lack of effect is not particularly surprising.

If it is not already apparent, the negative aspect to this approach, of course, is the availability of the comparative data from prior assessments. This type of comparative analysis is only available when more than one survey effort has been conducted over time and using all or at least some of the same assessment items. This is one of the reasons why a thorough item construction process should be followed during the first survey administration so that at least a majority of the survey questions will yield meaningful and important results now and in the future if used again. Between changing employees, roles and corporate agenda, it is often very difficult to retain the same survey design or process during subsequent administrations unless the system has become fully institutionalized. The energy and excitement that was behind the first survey effort has often been spent on resulting initiatives and/or other competing efforts by the time the second or third survey would be valuable. We have seen many organizations make effective use of a survey during a change effort, for example, only to decide a year later that a follow-up survey is either (a) too costly to find out that 'not enough' has changed, or (b) too burdensome to respond to on the part of employees or management in view of all of the other programmes and initiatives in progress.

The third and final type of comparative analysis for analysing survey results concerns the use of *external comparisons* or information, also known as bench-marking data to provide a referent point for ratings obtained. As we discussed in the Introduction, bench-marking is a process of comparing the results obtained from an internal survey with a predetermined external measure or bench mark to determine the relative standing of the organization's functions and operations. These external bench marks comprise the organization's top competitors and/or perhaps the best competitors in the same industry as well. Sometimes, companies in entirely different industries but with similar types of processes or issues facing them are used for comparison purposes. Regardless of the nature of the bench-marking database, the purpose of this type of analysis is to determine how well the current organization is doing in various areas relative to other firms that have collected the same or very similar information. At its most specific form, bench-marking has been used for documenting specific process and procedures for enhancing service and product quality (e.g., Camp, 1995; Spendolini, 1992). In other situations such as survey assessment efforts, the focus tends to be more on a comparison of issues such as satisfaction with compensation, benefits options offered by competitors, the level of training and education required for various jobs, the extent to which managers engage in specific types of behaviours (e.g., Johnson, 1996). In fact, bench-marking has become so popular that

131

some survey practitioners have gone as far as to promote the use of their bench-marking dataset, rather than allow for a custom-designed survey, as their primary competitive advantage. For some, a high degree of external comparability more than makes up for a lack of specificity and adaptability in the choice of content or questions assessed.

Some degree of external bench-marking is probably useful most of the time at a general level, particularly given the increasing tendency for organizations to span national boundaries and compete in different markets; however, some practitioners such as ourselves are concerned with an apparent overemphasis on this type of analysis approach. By itself, bench-marking organizational assessment survey data is likely to tell the analysis team very little, and provides for a rather weak set of interpretative statements. It may add some flavour and background to the results obtained, but it cannot and probably should not be used as the core set of analyses for any large-scale organizational survey effort. What is going on in one's own organization should be far more important and meaningful than how the data compare favourably or unfavourably with other companies at a more general level. We have seen far too many clients, for example, debate the merits of an external comparison or discredit some low survey rating obtained in their own company – such as a mean rating on a five-point scale of 1.96 for employee morale – because it was equally low or lower in other organizations included in the bench mark. From our perspective, if an organization has taken the time and money to conduct a survey properly, it should use the data gathered from that process and the relative degree of strengths and weaknesses as described earlier in this step as the basis for its analyses, interpretations, recommendations and action plans.

One final point regarding the use of bench-marking. As we stated in the Introduction, people often think of the word 'bench-marking' in terms of external indicators; however, internal survey ratings can be used as a bench mark too. Practitioners often refer to the results of an initial survey effort, for example, as being the bench mark or baseline for the future. Data from high-performing work teams, departments, functions, divisions, business units or entire countries can be used an internal bench marks as well. Of course, in the nomenclature used in this step, these would probably be classified as *comparisons by type* or *comparisons by time* but the idea across all three applications is generally the same – i.e., comparing one set of results to another to look for strengths and weaknesses to enhance the overall survey analysis picture.

CONTENT ANALYSIS OF WRITE-IN COMMENTS

The last stage in the survey analysis process concerns an entirely different type of data altogether – i.e., the written comments provided to various short-answer or open-ended questions such as: 'What is exciting about your job? What makes you come to work each day?' As discussed in Step 2, large-scale organizational survey efforts often include one or more of these types of more qualitative questions in conjunction with a series of quantitative ratings in order to provide greater depth and clarity during the analysis process. Unlike the myriad of available statistical options when working with raw numerical responses, the analysis of write-in comments is relatively simple and direct. The process most frequently employed here is called *content analysis* which basically means taking the individual idiosyncratic comments and opinions and converting them into a number of main categories or themes for interpretation purposes. If this procedure sounds familiar, it is because this is exactly the same process that is used by many OD or HRD professionals to analyse responses from focus groups, interviews and other types of qualitative data collection efforts. We have already introduced the use of this technique in Step 2 with respect to generating survey item content and providing feedback based on information-gathering during meetings with organizational members.

Content analysis is a relatively straightforward process, and requires no special skills other than the ability to conceptualize and sort responses based on a number of categories or themes. Here are some sample write-in comments taken from several different large-scale survey efforts in response to the question 'What are the blocks, hindrances, barriers that prevent you from doing your work effectively?':

> Change is happening so fast and there is too much of it. So many managers are inexperienced in their new roles when I need information.

> The cronyism and sexism dictates advancement far more than do ability and performance. This is still a white male-dominated institution.

> It's quite appalling that this organization still condones high-handed and humiliating managerial style, cronyism and, unfortunately, is not always kind toward people of colour.

> The bureaucraticness. I'm filling out this survey under lights that blew out over three weeks ago and though reported have still not been fixed.

> Lack of any forward planning, no business plan seems to last more than six months. No investment is planned until equipment is worn out or sudden events require it, for example, new safety legislation.

> Customer service should be more proactive and less reactive; this company seems to manage with a fire drill mentality.

133

Departments which do not like or trust one another mainly due to upbringing, education or class.

Comments and criticism are discouraged in this company and are often held against people who make them. We have a long way to go, and a few 'feel good' meetings and employee surveys are not going to mean as much as positive and honest action.

Management is blatant about favouritism, not allowing for others to learn or advance to the same level of growth or promotion.

A very sad lack of management that we can respect. We are appalled at the way we are treated as staff and at the seeming lack of understanding of our feelings of helplessness as we see the erosion of our standards and ways of treating each other.

Staff attitude of 'If you don't want the job, there are many others who do'.

Morale went out of the window months ago and yet we are issued a mission statement which probably cost quite a bit of money and would be just as appropriately written on the side of an ice-cream truck.

Frequent management U-turns about our role and responsibilities. Lack of understanding by managers of what we actually have to do to carry out our jobs effectively.

Due to cuts, closures and reorganizations I no longer have an experienced or accessible senior manager I can turn to.

During the merger senior management lied to employees and were not concerned about our jobs. They did not help those of us who lost our jobs and had to find other employment. They were only concerned about themselves and were not the least bit sensitive toward the rest of us.

The most frustrating thing is our lack of reliable equipment. Our PCs are always giving us problems, the printers are always breaking, we are spending unnecessary hours making up work we lost because of bad equipment. Please give us good equipment so we can do our jobs more efficiently and be happier coming to work!

Changes are made overnight without advising us and without any training provided, yet we are expected to bumble along without a glitch. When our departments were merged no effort was made to bring people together and make us all feel comfortable.

Marriage leave taken away; no Christmas bonus; benefits are terrible, job security a major problem. Always worried about losing my job – can't sleep at night!

I have an enormous additional workload with reduced support. Experience, expertise and goodwill count for nothing anymore.

The only negative aspect of the content analysis process is that it often requires a significant amount of time and effort to transcribe or input the comments into a computer form for manipulation (e.g., cutting and pasting, tabulating, sort, etc.), particularly with optical scan or pen and paper survey administration methods. Some data collection systems can record the information directly in electronic form (e.g., on-line web sites or voice-response units), but these methods often have other difficulties associated with their use including reduced levels of par-ticipation, unease regarding confidentiality and occasional problems in transfer-ring the data obtained through these methods to other computer formats. In any case, regardless of the method of administration used, the analysis of quantita-tive data is laborious and time-consuming. The richness of the information obtained, however, often more than makes up for the extra effort involved, which is one of the reasons why these types of questions are so popular in survey efforts. Before describing the specific process by which to conduct a content analysis, there are two decisions regarding the use of the write-ins obtained that must first be understood because the outcomes have important implications for how the data are analysed and subsequently interpreted.

First and foremost is the question of using a sample versus a census of the comments obtained. Should the content analysis be based on all of the individual write-ins obtained or should it be completed using only a random or perhaps stratified random sample? One's initial reaction might be to use all of the data available; however, given the tight time constraints involved in the survey analy-sis process and the voluminous amount of information gathered with such methods – sometimes several pages of text per individual particularly if there are multiple questions or large numbers of respondents to the survey – more often than not the decision is to use a representative sample of the comments obtained. This is not a problem because (a) an appropriate sample set of com-ments is likely to be rich enough to provide meaningful and insightful informa-tion, and (b) the entire set of responses can always by coded later after the results have already been communicated at the first or second level. Thus, the general rule of thumb here is a 20 per cent sample of the total responses, i.e., for a survey with 2,000 returns, you would use 400 write-ins for the content analysis process. The only other concern besides size when choosing a sample is the extent to which various business units, functions or countries are adequately represented. In some situations, for example, it might be desirable to ensure that responses from different locations are appropriately represented, particularly if there may be differences evident in other areas.

The second decision in the content analysis process is whether or not the results obtained are going to be fully integrated with the other more quantitative analyses produced. If integration of these different sources of information is key to the final interpretation and presentation, which is highly recommended although not always possible for a variety of reasons, then the content coding categories of themes used should match as closely as possible the framework and/or variables used for the conceptual and comparative analyses results. The write-ins should be classified and selected in such a way as to provide additional support and elucidation regarding the key issues and themes identified in the numerical responses. However, in situations where the write-in questions were asked regarding very specific topics, there is not adequate time to integrate the findings into a comprehensive whole, or certain individuals are wary of using write-ins because of their qualitative nature, then the content coding categories should reflect the actual themes inherent in the comments themselves whatever they may be. For example, in the first situation the comments might be coded according to the 12 boxes in the Burke–Litwin model (e.g., leadership, culture, mission, motivation, systems, etc.) whereas in the second case the themes might be more specific such as 'job security', 'upgrade technology', 'increase staff levels', 'reduce paperwork', or 'get better managers'. The choice here is usually based on a combination of time, resources, the types of questions asked and the expectations of the client regarding results.

With these decisions taken, the following stages describe the content analysis process itself as it is usually performed:

1. Identification of the total comment pool available for analysis (i.e., sample or census).
2. Initial examination of the responses for general tone, potential content themes (assuming main classification categories have not already been identified from a conceptual model or prior analyses) and good representative sample quotes for use in reporting (depending on level of quantitative and qualitative data integration needed).
3. Formal classification of all write-in responses from pool into content categories or themes. It is not considered good practice to classify the same comment into different categories concurrently (because it gets listed and counted twice this way); however, it is acceptable to break up a given individual's comments into separate parts or points and classify these in different themes accordingly.
4. Continuous refinement and adjustment to content themes (e.g., modification of categories and/or addition of subcategories) as needed.
5. Once coding is complete, tabulation of the number of responses per category or theme into frequencies so that the relative importance of each issue can be determined.

Table 5.9 provides an example of what the result of this entire process might look like based on a sample of 354 responses in a larger survey effort.

Table 5.9 Sample content analysis results

What is exciting about your job? What makes you come to work each day?	Number of responses	Percentage of total
Successfully helping customers	110	31
Challenging work	76	21
Teamwork among colleagues	60	17
Variety and diversity of work	43	12
Opportunity to contribute	25	7
Nothing but the pay cheque	24	7
Developing new skills	16	5
Total	354	

CHECKLIST FOR STEP 5

1. Determine the role of statistics.
   - Use those in which you are skilled and use an expert for those in which you are not.
   - Carefully consider using tests of significance.

2. Remember that timing is very important.
   Prepare the following in advance (as analysis and interpretation are usually allotted the *shortest* amount of time of all seven steps):
   - Make sure that data entry system is fully operational and has been tested.
   - Install and test all data analysis software.
   - Write and test initial analysis code using sample data.
   - Obtain results from previous surveys for bench-marking purposes.
   - Manage the clients' expectations and anxiety regarding issues with the data collected.
   - Prepare a comprehensive and thoughtful data analysis plan.
   - Develop a framework or outline of the final survey report.

3. The six stages for analysis and interpretation.
   - Data entry – formally enter results into some sort of database.
   - Data preparation – check for missing, incomplete or partially completed responses; duplicate responses from same individual; problematic and/or intentional response patterns; incorrect use of scales; negatively worded items; inconsistencies in responses to similar items; damaged forms; compute malfunctions.
   - Item-level analysis.
   - Conceptual-level analysis.
   - Comparative analysis.
   - Content analysis of write-in comments.

6 Delivering the findings

It shall be a vexation only to understand the report.

Isaiah

Imagine the following scene. You are at work one day and you are called into a meeting that your manager feels will be useful and informative to you. So you put aside whatever mission important work you are engaged in and head off for the meeting. Realizing that the meeting is just about to start you gingerly walk down the hall, open the large oak door and enter the cavernous boardroom. The myriad of armchairs are arranged in a crescent shape around a deep mahogany-coloured table. You take a seat on the left-hand side of the table near the front. During the next five minutes or so, several other individuals, some of whom you know, and some of whom are from a consulting firm, shuffle into the room and take their seats as well. A professional-looking individual enters the room, goes to the front of the table, pulls out a large report and starts speaking in a language you have never heard before. You do not know what this person is saying. After the first few minutes of the presentation, you begin to vacillate between feeling bored and uninterested in what is being presented since you cannot understand it anyway, and experiencing anxiety every time the other individuals in the room nod their heads in understanding and astonishment at the speaker's comments. You then ask yourself, what does this have to do with me and my job anyway? Why am I wasting my time here when I could be doing something important? And why are these consultants getting paid big bucks for this nonsense?

This is an exaggerated version of what can and often does happen during the presentation of a complex or extended set of survey results when the delivery process has not been well managed. People in the audience can easily get confused, overloaded and/or lost in their own issues and anxieties resulting in your message not being heard at all. Keep in mind that the fundamental purpose of any survey report is to provide a clear, accurate and appropriately detailed picture of the organization which allows others to plan for action. In other words, while complex conceptual models, interpretations and causal relationships are useful additions to a survey report and well worth pursuing, they should not be considered the *definitive* word or the *end result* of a survey feedback effort. Rather, these analyses and interpretations should help the end-user understand and make use of the larger dataset collected. It is probably not possible to ensure that all aspects of a presentation of survey findings will be crystal clear and easily understood by everyone on the receiving end, but an effective survey presentation and accompanying report can have a significant impact on the perceived success or failure of the assessment effort regardless of the nature of the actual results obtained. The purpose of this step, then, is to discuss the issues, options and applications of presenting and delivering to a variety of audiences the survey results and findings obtained.

However, we would point out that despite our use of the term 'delivery' in connection with survey feedback, it is often good practice (particularly at higher levels of management) to approach a results-oriented presentation from a more facilitative than expert perspective – i.e., as a 'working session' wherein the results are presented to a group of end-users and then a diagnosis and/or series of recommendations are created jointly through discussion and debate of the issues raised. This more action-research related approach is often useful for building enhanced levels of commitment and support behind whatever action plans may result from a survey effort. This method of delivering feedback, however, also means that the survey results themselves need to be highly accessible and easily understood.

UNDERSTANDING THE ROLL-OUT PROCESS

Perhaps the first and most important element to understand when beginning work on the first survey report or presentation is the roll-out process – i.e., the method and sequence by which the results are to be presented to all those involved – and the role and expectations regarding this initial set of findings. This, of course, takes us back to many of the issues discussed in the first few steps on the subject of survey planning and objectives. What were the primary objectives of the survey? Who will be receiving exactly which results and under what time frame? How is the information provided intended to be used? Since each survey report itself is in some ways the *second half of the analysis process*, the answers to all these questions have a significant impact on the nature of the first and all subsequent reports generated.

In organizations where a survey effort has been initiated in response to some large-scale change effort or new strategic directive, the results are intended usually to be used at several different levels starting with a global picture of the main trends and themes to senior management. This is often followed by more specific regional, directorate, departmental or functional reports for first, second,

Table 6.1   Sample survey roll-out plan

Target group	Time frame from close of administration	Objectives and issues involved
Survey sponsor	1–2 weeks	• Present initial findings including raw data, trends, conceptual variables, key relationships • Adjust highlights and areas for emphasis before moving to more formal presentation
Executive committee	3–4 weeks	• Formal presentation of key findings, themes and interpretations • Focus on conveying information in what is often a very short period of time (e.g., 15 minutes to 1 hour)
Senior management	4–6 weeks	• Formal presentation to all of upper management (e.g., top 200 executives, etc.) group to convey key messages and gain commitment to and support of changes that may result • Focus on revised version of main issues and interpretations presented to Executive Committee • Timing (1 hour versus 1 day) and format (large group all at once versus small groups at different times) used for delivery may vary considerably
Middle management	4–8 weeks	• Specific reports of findings based on individual actionable units, departments or functions, or managers • Results must be provided with attention to existing time frames to be used for planning and objective-setting purposes • May or may not contain extensive interpretation and/or customized conceptual modelling or other types of advanced analysis for their particular set of responses
All employees	4–16 weeks	• General messages regarding survey objectives and highlights of findings • Some organizations provide all item-level responses at this stage, others prefer to provide summary-level data only • Senior-level commentary and/or response to results is recommended but not always available • Timing can affect acceptance and credibility of results presented (i.e., the sooner the better)

third and sometimes even lower middle management ranks. In addition, a 'paired down' version of the results describing the overall findings and perhaps some commentary or a discussion of intended responses from senior leadership is often issued to all employees via a corporate newsletter, special publication, video or other means within a short period as well. Table 6.1 provides an overview of the components and issues of a roll-out plan of this nature. This same type of roll-out process is often followed by institutionalized survey systems as well, particularly when they are intended to be used for performance management and objective-setting processes. Top-level reports regarding the state of the organization for senior leadership, specific actionable reports for

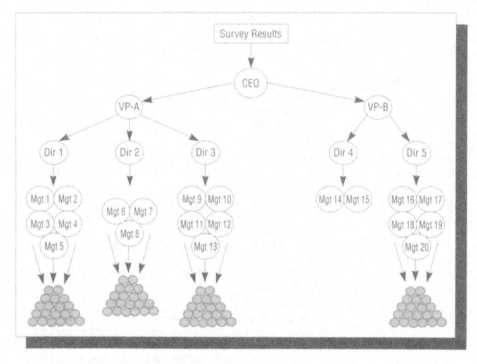

Figure 6.1   Cascading survey feedback delivery process

managers to use in their planning process, and a comprehensive message for employees. In a large-scale organizational survey of this type, it is possible to provide not only reports for every department based on average ratings by its members, but also one that compares how several different departments rate one another in a variety of areas such as co-operation, integration, communication and internal service quality. Figure 6.1 illustrates this cascading approach to survey feedback delivery.

In comparison, there are other types of survey efforts that may be more limited to a top-level report only by design (e.g., by including very limited demographic questions in the instrument). In these situations, unlike in the top-down approach, it is probably best to be as comprehensive as possible regarding results and interpretation presented to the end-users. These survey assessments applications are typically aimed at gathering information relating to a specific topic (e.g., effectiveness of communication systems, use of performance appraisal systems, general morale and satisfaction, etc.) for consideration by some action-oriented group or task force.

The final point here concerns the issue of timing itself. As we stated in Step 5, most people's interest in seeing the results of the survey effort start to rise from the moment they complete and return their questionnaire until after about two months at which point it begins to sharply decline. This means that, as with the data analysis stage, timing is very important during the report preparation and delivery stage as well. What can be considered an acceptable time frame varies from one organization and its particular culture to another, and from one individual to another (based on such variables as relevance and importance at the time of the survey, and perceived ability for change on the part of management); however, the level of interest, commitment and value associated with the survey results obtained does tend to follow this pattern most of the time. The practitioner or survey team therefore needs to take enough time in the analysis and reporting stages to provide a clear set of messages in an accessible medium for the intended audiences. Whatever the time required for the report delivery and roll-out process, however, this information should be clearly communicated to all potential end-users (including employees) so that people know when they can expect to receive some feedback regarding the survey effort. As we emphasized in Step 3, communication is very important during this portion of the process as well.

PREPARING THE SURVEY REPORT

The objectives, timing and audience of a survey report will have a significant impact on the format and contents of the materials ultimately generated but there are, none the less, a number of standard elements that are part and parcel of almost any type of survey report (see Table 6.2). The form and function of each of these is described in detail below.

Table 6.2 Elements of the survey report

1. Cover page
2. Executive summary
3. Introduction to the study
4. Review of preliminary research
5. Method of research
6. Survey results
7. Conclusions and recommendations
8. Appendix

Source: Adapted and expanded from Rea and Parker (1992).

143

COVER PAGE

The first and probably most obvious element of any survey report is the cover page. The cover page does not have to be overly complicated; however, it does have to convey the key information necessary to differentiate it from the myriad of other reports, studies, handbooks, manuals and other assorted reams of paper that are typically generated by and for organizations. Even if the information contained within is highly intuitive, a report without a cover is often seen as just another pile of paper waiting to be thrown out. Unlike the old adage, a book *is* often judged by its cover and, therefore, the look and feel of this element are also important. If time and budget allow it is often useful to consult someone with expertise in designing cover graphics to help you put together a look that is both easy to read and user friendly. In terms of content, the minimum items to include here consist of:

- a title that is both clear and succinct and that identifies the subject or content area of the study
- the names, affiliations and complete contact information for each of the principal authors
- the date and status of the report delivered – i.e., initial draft, revised report, final version for the management committee or senior management, etc.

EXECUTIVE SUMMARY

The next element, which is the first content-related section of the report, is the executive summary. The purpose of this section is to provide a short and concise summary of the main findings, themes, relationships and issues identified in the data analysis and interpretation phase. Often somewhere between three to six pages in length, this section is designed to convey the most important messages to the reader in a quick and easily digestible manner. It should be thorough enough so that if someone only has time to read the summary itself, they will still be relatively well informed about the main findings obtained. Even if the report is not going to be presented to executives, this condensed version of the findings is very useful to have available to anyone picking up the report now or in the future. To this end, the executive summary is usually based on an item-level analysis such as the highest and lowest questions, with some elements of conceptual and/or trend analyses woven in as well. Sometimes this is done solely through the use of explanatory text (as in the following example):

> Employees were less positive about the organization's communication of strategic plans, plans for growth and success and how their organization differs from others with the same services.

Also, employees expressed concerns about the organization's interest in employees in terms of their welfare and people's attitudes toward their work. Employees do not experience open communication in the workplace. Specifically, they do not feel comfortable expressing their thoughts and opinions openly and do not see knowledge being transferred throughout the organization in a timely manner.

Regarding leadership, employees expressed little trust in senior management. They do not see senior management as inspirational or in touch with employees at their level.

Finally, organizational members gave the lowest ratings on items concerning restructuring and reorganization. Employees do not think that the rationale behind structural changes and reorganization have been effectively communicated (lowest rated item 2.9). They also do not believe that structural changes have been effectively managed.

In other cases, a graphic or model might be used to help summarize the issues (see Figure 6.2 for an example of the latter). The executive summary usually ends with an overview of the details to follow in the rest of the report. In some instances, when the audience might be in need of a bit more direction, it may be appropriate to include some additional interpretive elements and possible

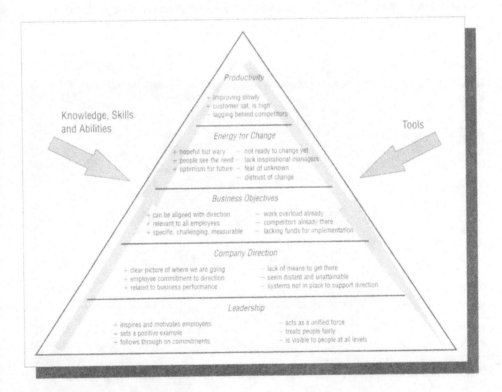

Figure 6.2   Sample executive summary

recommendations as well. As we have noted earlier, however, this type of highly directive information is less likely to encourage active participation and internalization on the part of the recipient, resulting in a potentially weakened impact of the results.

INTRODUCTION TO THE STUDY

The third main section in a survey report is the formal introduction to the study itself. This is where the relevant and important background and contextual information is presented for the end-user. It should be written with the assumption that this section is the true entry point to the rest of the document (i.e., in case the executive summary is removed). To this end, topics to be described here include:

- who participated in the study (e.g., the characteristics of the survey respondents including the rate of return, some detail regarding background information, whether the survey was a census or a sample – see Figure 6.3)
- why the survey was conducted (e.g., provide the problem statement or issues that led to the use of a survey, as well as the specific survey objectives)

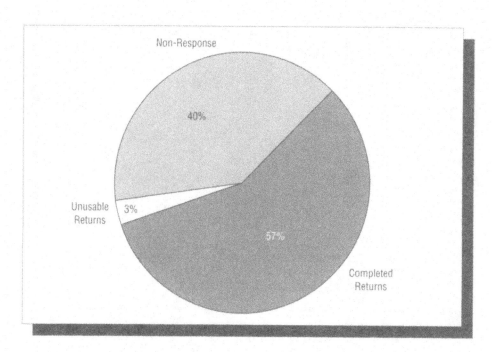

Figure 6.3 Survey response rate information

146

- when the survey was conducted (e.g., the total length of time made available for responses including the open and close dates, be sure to note the use of initial communications and follow-up reminders during administration as well)
- how the survey was conducted (e.g., some detail on the method(s) of administration chosen and why).

Note that this section is not meant to provide a complete listing of all the details of the survey process. This will be done later on in the report. Rather, enough specific information should be provided in a relatively short series of pages so that the validity and credibility of the assessment process, and therefore the findings obtained, are readily demonstrated to the reader.

REVIEW OF PRELIMINARY RESEARCH

With the introduction complete, it is now appropriate to provide a significantly greater level of detail regarding the level of preliminary work that was conducted and used to design and develop the current instrument (and conceptual model if appropriate). Since this section is often used more as a reference tool than a main source of information regarding the survey results *per se*, it should contain as much detail as is available and relevant. Elements that would be relevant here include:

- supporting information available on the nature of the specific problems facing the organization that prompted the survey effort
- relevant background information relating to other organizational change efforts, strategic initiatives, restructuring, financial performance and cultural issues
- summaries of prior surveys, research studies conducted, consulting projects or other types of written reports related to this initiative
- an overview of the methodology and results highlights of any focus groups, interviews or related preliminary data collection
- information on any pilot surveys conducted, test cases and associated refinement efforts used to finalize the instrument
- source information and descriptions of any key articles, books, guides or other related external references used; the nature of the role of any related professional expertise or other types of outside sources consulted
- information regarding main areas of consensus and conflict regarding key issues and decisions made.

147

METHOD OF RESEARCH

The purpose of this section is to move the discussion forward again by describing the survey administration process and subsequent analysis plan in significant detail. Once again, since this section is more likely to be used to answer specific questions rather than provide the results themselves, it should be as complete and informative as possible. Mirroring what was covered briefly in the introduction to the study, information to provide here includes a detailed outline of the administration methods:

- who was involved in the design of the instrument and what their roles were
- who administered the instrument (internal staff, external consultants)
- how employees received the instrument (describe all methods if more than one was used)
- when and what types of pre-survey communication efforts were used
- when and what types of follow-up measures were employed
- who was involved in crafting the communications
- how the sample was selected and verified as being appropriate and accurate
- how names and contact information for the sample or census were identified and adjusted when necessary
- how returns were tracked and processed.

Also relevant is an overview and definition for each of the statistics and approaches used during the data analysis and interpretation stage. Of course, if any write-in questions are to be reported, this section would also include an overview of the process by which the comments were content analysed (and integrated into the findings or analysed separately) as well.

DETAILED SURVEY RESULTS

After all the background, supporting documentation and details on administration, it is time to present the detailed survey findings to the end-user. As one might expect, this section is the longest in any survey feedback report. This is because it will usually contain the following elements:

- summary scores for all grouping variables used (e.g., based on the organization's core values, management competencies, strategic objectives, or some set of key conceptual variables based on an organizational model, framework or the results of a complex statistical analysis)
- means and/or percentages for each individual item included in the survey (the inclusion of the specific wording used for each item is highly recommended as well)

- comparison values and/or delta or change scores if relevant (e.g., between a prior survey and the present one, or between the larger organizational norm and the current one for some business unit, region, function, or department)
- content analysis of focus group findings (including themes, frequencies and sample quotes for each)
- a subsection containing the complete responses to all descriptive or background items asked.

Approaches to how the information is presented in this section may vary considerably given the myriad of graphic and reporting software available today (some practitioners prefer frequency tables or presenting data displaying percentage of favourable responses as described in Step 5), but the basic idea is to provide all the information in a comprehensive but user-friendly manner. This means displaying the data using a combination of formats such as tables, bar charts, pie charts, line graphs, 2 × 2 matrices, and even model-related graphics.

Our preference with regard to reporting detailed survey results of this nature is to provide means scores in the form of bar charts grouped by specific content areas. Aside from the bar itself, these charts will always contain at least (a) the end points of the rating scale used, (b) the specific wording of the question and its item number on the instrument, and (c) a numeric form of the mean score as well. Other options include a comparison point (such as the prior year's score, or the norm for the larger organization when using lower level reports, or perhaps even an external bench-mark score if particularly relevant and meaningful) as well as some indication of the total range of responses obtained (e.g., using a line or proving a percentile score, or listing the highest and lowest scores for a given area). Figures 6.4 and 6.5 provide sample charts depicting these relatively basic types of displays.

The best approach to providing detailed findings is to present the primary results obtained, with only one or two other types of comparative data points included if absolutely necessary. Since the primary objective of most survey reports is to convey information rather than specify a complete solution, it is often better to keep interpretation to a minimum. Too much data and/or too much interpretation in this section can make the results less clear and subsequently diffuse their impact. While these points have already been made in the data analysis and interpretation process in Step 5, it is worth repeating them here since they can also affect the overall delivery of the survey findings. Similarly, although at times it may be tempting to display all the responses obtained using a series of cuts by important demographic variables such as region, gender, function or ethnicity, the survey practitioner is required to take a stand here and concentrate on the results as much as possible. When these types of cuts are figured too early in the process it presents two problems: (a) potential

149

DESIGNING AND USING ORGANIZATIONAL SURVEYS

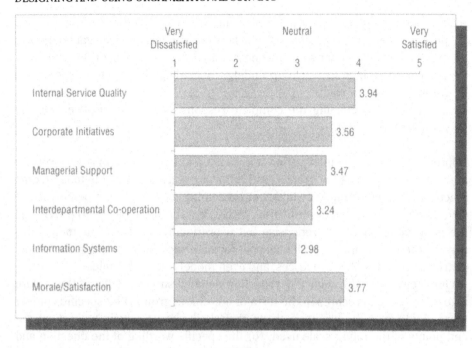

Figure 6.4   Sample bar chart with summary scores for main content areas

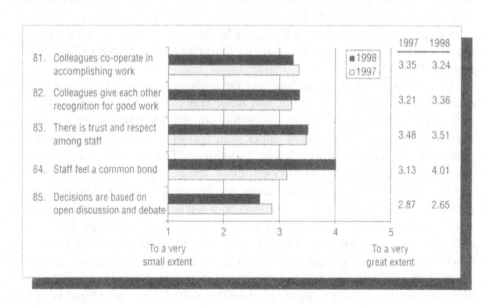

Figure 6.5   Sample item-level chart with comparative data provided

150

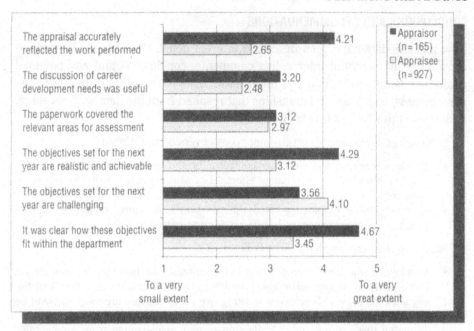

The appraisal accurately
reflected the work performed — 4.21 / 2.65

The discussion of career
development needs was useful — 3.20 / 2.48

The paperwork covered the
relevant areas for assessment — 3.12 / 2.97

The objectives set for the next
year are realistic and achievable — 4.29 / 3.12

The objectives set for the next
year are challenging — 3.56 / 4.10

It was clear how these objectives
fit within the department — 4.67 / 3.45

Appraisor (n = 165)
Appraisee (n = 927)

1   2   3   4   5
To a very   To a very
small extent   great extent

Figure 6.6   Sample chart comparing responses for two specific groups

isolationistic and subsequent dismissal of various sets of findings if they tend to hold for only certain groups, and (b) data overload and disengagement with the findings. If the objectives of the survey are to assess the impact of some set of interventions on several different groups then this type of approach is probably warranted. For the sample data displayed in Figure 6.6, for example, it is preferable to provide the average responses from both the appraisee and appraisor perspectives in order to highlight the clear differences in perspectives of utility of the appraisal process between the two groups of users.

Since the purpose of the survey effort in Figure 6.6 was to assess and respond to these discrepancies, providing a total summary score of both sets of responses would probably have obscured these results (particularly given the differences in sample sizes). In most cases, however, this level of comparative information is best left to future analyses, then if necessary, a summary of the general trends only; and at the very least a low-key listing in the appendix so that the overall findings and trends can be fully examined, understood and acted on before people move into the more detailed and complex data.

CONCLUSIONS AND RECOMMENDATIONS

Now that the data have been described in great detail, the end-user is ready to consider your insightful interpretive comments, conclusions and any potential recommendations for action you might have. This is the place to highlight the main themes, trends and relationships that resulted from the data analysis stage. Examples of this type of information might include:

Summary of differences: direct customer contact versus internal staff

- Employees with direct customer contact indicated greater understanding of the mission and goals of the change effort. They also rated senior leadership more positively.
- However, these employees rated the company's structure, employee support systems and their managers' behaviour more negatively.

Summary of differences: length of service

- Employees who have been working in the company for two years or less are far more likely to be optimistic about positive change occurring as a result of the organization survey. Employees working five years or more are more likely to be pessimistic.
- While all three categories of leadership (senior management team, region/division senior management and area directors) are rated highly by new employees, a clear difference in the ratings given to area directors and other senior management develops quickly after that and persists throughout each length of service category. Ratings of leadership are lowest among those employees who have worked in the company for a longer period of time (three years or more).
- Employee morale, and feelings of empowerment and satisfaction decline as length of service increases. Ratings of the job itself remain relatively consistent, however, lending weight to the validity of external causes for the drop in satisfaction.

Besides highlighting key trends, conceptual models and advanced statistics often influence the contents of this section as well, although this may or may not be made apparent to the reader. Figure 6.7 and Table 6.3 provide an example of how one of these more complex analyses based on the results of a multiple regression procedure can be used to describe key levers for change in a report. As you will see, the numerics involved in this analysis are not presented for the reader (compare this presentation, for example, to the more complete but perhaps less easily understood model detailed in Figure 5.5).

Regardless of the level of complexity used in the analysis process, however, this section also provides the survey team (and ultimately the sponsor as well) with the opportunity to recommend various alternative courses of action as a result of the issues identified. There is often some level of repetition of highest and lowest ratings, areas which were mentioned most often or most aggressively in the write-in responses or those pertaining to specific content areas of interest. The only other main elements that might also be included in this section are

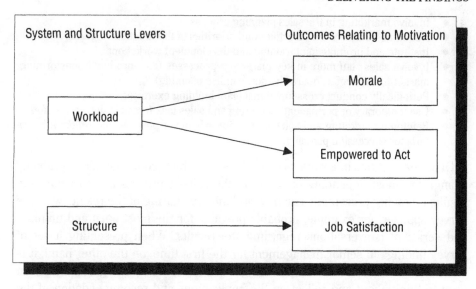

Figure 6.7   Key levers for change

Table 6.3   Key levers for change: individual performance and motivation

Since the motivation section of the survey contains a number of different questions pertaining to various aspects such as morale and feelings of empowerment, these specific items were examined independently to identify key levers for change. The following graphics represent the primary levers (i.e., the single most important predictors) for enhancing each aspect of employee motivation.

Descriptions of predictive items	
Workload	*Structure*
Q91. Branches have sufficient staff support during peak periods.	Q48. Structure is decentralized; people are encouraged to take initiative and have authority to act.
Q92. Information gets to the right people at the right time.	Q50. Structure helps business performance.
Q93. People are rewarded for serving their customers to a very great extent.	Q49. The current organizational structure helps different departments co-operate and work together effectively.
Q98. I do far less paperwork than I used to 12 months ago.	Q51. Employees have the authority and latitude they need to serve their customers.
Q99. Formal systems and processes enhance our ability to work effectively.	

some additional information regarding future roll-out plans for lower levels in the organization as well as possible opportunities for future research or study. Here are some sample recommendations that can be included in this type of report:

Structure: implement a series of devices to enhance marketing and sales integration

- Integrate annual business plans so that there are overlapping objectives.

153

- Involve marketing in the sales planning process.
- Negotiate quarterly the objectives and priorities of the functions together.
- Institute and promote joint training and development workshops.
- Involve sales staff more in key marketing processes (e.g., product brainstorming, marketing strategies, quarterly merchandise planning).
- Periodically conduct cross-functional team-building exercises.
- Use temporary or permanent marketing and sales task forces to get work done.
- Reinforce marketing and sales integration whenever possible and reflect it in criteria for succession planning.

Of all the sections in a survey report, however, the recommendations probably change the most depending on when in the roll-out process and to whom the results are being presented. The first preliminary sharing of the results with the survey sponsor, for example, probably provides for the most open and uninhibited series of conversations regarding the results. When presenting a set of survey findings to senior management for the first time, on the other hand, it is often prudent to avoid overemphasizing this section since this group will often want to think about and reflect on the implications and recommendation of the results themselves. The conclusions and recommendations presented to this group are likely to be very different in tone (and perhaps even in content) from what this group might want communicated to all employees in some type of corporate-wide document. Similarly, in many individual reporting situations such as departmental or functional groupings, the purpose of a feedback presentation may be to develop a series of recommendations and action planning steps based on a joint discussion and interpretation of the data displayed in the detailed survey results section. On the other hand, we have seen departments in some organizations take a completely analysed and fully interpreted set of survey results for their specific area, and create a totally independent communication piece with their own conclusions and recommendations for distribution to their people.

APPENDIX

The final element to a standard survey report is the appendix (or if more than one the appendices). The appendix is probably the easiest section to write (after the cover page), and it is likely to be rather large in size. This is where the practitioner provides any and all additional materials that might be relevant to the survey effort. The appendix usually comprises the following kinds of items:

- sample copy of the survey instrument used (if no hard copy was used, then a listing of the specific items and associated scales would be substituted)
- copies of all important communications (e.g., cover letter mailed with survey, reminder and follow-up letters, postcards, information sheets provided, etc.)

154

- list of key contributors to various stages of the process (e.g., task force members, survey sponsor and team members, participants in item design focus group and/or interviews, etc.)
- content analysis information of write-in comments (if not included in the detailed survey results section, or if more detail is warranted)
- any other supplementary documents such as additional listings of numbers by specific groups, etc.

BALANCING EXPECTATIONS AND REALITY

The presentation and delivery of feedback results is in and of itself a relatively straightforward process, and assuming that most of the issues and components described above are adequately addressed, there is one more set of issues that needs to be discussed. These pertain primarily to the ethics and responsibilities inherent in the survey feedback process itself.

First, survey practitioners and the survey team should realize that any data collection process, regardless of the content to which it is directed, has the potential to raise anxiety and fear on the part of respondents, end-users and even the survey sponsor. Between the formal costs and resources associated with the conduct of a survey effort and the emotional energy and heightened awareness and expectations of a response to organizational concerns among respondents, it is very likely that the results will be met with some resistance and anxiety when presented and, even, further on in the process. Therefore, the survey practitioner needs to help manage and work the client, sponsor and/or end-users through these issues and concerns in a productive rather than destructive manner. This means creating survey reports that temper negative findings and areas for change with positives and strengths (even when there may appear to be few or none). It also means preparing the client for difficult ratings and helping the client to accept the results for what they are rather than allowing them to defensively dismiss the ratings as being invalid, unimportant or beyond management's ability to respond.

A second issue here regarding professional conduct concerns the extent to which the survey practitioner maintains his or her integrity in the delivery process regarding (a) the reality and validity of the interpretation of the data obtained, and (b) adherence to the original contract regarding the confidentiality of responses. It should be clear from the discussion above and in Step 5 that there is never a perfectly correct interpretation for any given set of survey data, but it is possible for people to completely misinterpret, intentionally obscure, and even potentially falsify certain types of findings and outcomes based on their own idiosyncratic 'view' of the results. The latter is probably not too common in

155

practice, nevertheless people often put their own 'spin' on a set of survey results when preparing to convey them to others in the organization, particularly in situations where a powerful group other than the survey team (or practitioner) takes control of the communication and/or action planning process. In these situations, the onus is on the survey professional to ensure that end-users and employees will receive an appropriate set of findings and/or interpretation which accurately reflect the data obtained at least on some level. It is only fair that everyone who participated should receive some acknowledgement and feedback for their efforts and that the feedback should be accurate, meaningful and easy to understand.

Similarly, it is the ethical responsibility of the survey practitioner to protect the level of confidentiality of the individual responses obtained regardless of the pressures placed on them by the client or other powerful groups interested in exploiting the survey results. For example, if respondents were promised confidentiality at the level of a 20-person minimum per individual report, then all requests exceeding this limit (e.g., for a department with 11 responses) from the client, survey sponsor or even senior management should be rejected. The only solution here would be to provide the data in question combined with some other smaller set to reach the minimum allowed. Once again, this is one of the benefits of using an external agent to collect and analyse the survey responses because it provides a buffer between senior management and the data protection mechanisms. For many external survey experts, the only way their raw survey data may be obtained is through a successful legal action.

CHECKLIST FOR STEP 6

1. Determine the roll-out process.

This means deciding on the method and sequence by which the results are to be presented to all those involved (see Table 6.1) for a sample survey roll-out plan). Usually rolling-out results includes some kind of cascading process. At a minimum, however, the following elements should be considered in any roll-out plan:
- Who is the target group who will receive the survey results?
- What is the time frame from the close of administration to reporting?
- What are the objectives and issues involved in rolling-out survey results?

2. Prepare the survey report.

A completed survey report should contain each of the following elements:
- cover page: name of survey, date of survey, creator(s) of survey

- executive summary: brief narrative of findings in summary form
- introduction to the study: who participated, when and why the survey was conducted
- review of preliminary research: background information, methods overview, research
- method of research: how the survey was designed and how the results were collected
- detailed survey results: exact findings of survey usually by item or summary dimension
- conclusions and recommendations: recommended actions based on findings
- appendix: cover letters, the survey instruments itself, list of contributors.

3. Balance expectations and reality.
   - Always remember that any data collection process has the potential to raise anxiety and fear on the part of respondents, end-users and even the survey sponsor.
   - Maintain your integrity in the delivery process regarding (a) the reality and validity of the interpretation of the data obtained, and (b) adherence to the original contract concerning the confidentiality of responses.
   - Protect the confidentiality of the individual responses obtained regardless of the pressures by the client or other powerful groups interested in exploiting the survey results.

7 Learning into action

Knowledge must come through action.

Sophocles

Despite the continued popularity of consultants promoting change management initiatives in organizations, there is considerable evidence to suggest that most such efforts fail to have any noticeable, let alone a lasting, impact on the company. A 1992 survey of 300 electronics companies, for example, indicated that 63 per cent of those organizations implementing new total quality management (TQM) efforts had failed to yield improvements in their level of product defects (Schaffer and Thomson, 1992). Similarly poor outcomes have been reported for other types of large-scale interventions such as re-engineering, business process improvement and culture change efforts (e.g., Kotter, 1995; Spector and Beer, 1994; Trahant and Burke, 1996). There are certainly likely to be a host of contributing factors to this high failure rate, but one variable in particular is the extent to which the organization truly embraces and supports the process or methodology of choice.

Many organizations undertake a variety of large-scale corporate initiatives, including survey assessments, in an effort to stay current with the latest 'management fad' without having put enough time or thought into how or why a particular change or process might be beneficial to the system. These haphazard approaches to change management often result in the communication of a 'new strategic direction' every year or two and, in some cases, potentially conflicting initiatives and messages within a few months of each other. Termed 'the flavour of the month' by some of the more cynical commentators in the field (e.g., Adams, 1996), besides confusing employees, frequent changes often prevent these initiatives from taking hold in the larger culture as well. In fact, this tendency towards following suit (e.g., 'let's get some of that 360–degree feedback stuff') is one of the primary reasons why many employees in organizations today approach most new corporate initiatives or directives with apathy and/or cynicism. In short, there is often insufficient follow-through to make change happen and to make it endure.

159

Not surprisingly, these same issues and concerns are mirrored in organizational survey efforts as well, particularly in this final phase of the process – i.e., transferring ownership and taking action based on the results obtained. Many people, including some survey practitioners, consider the delivery of the results in and of themselves to be the end-point in the process; however, the fact is that this step actually determines how much impact a survey will actually have on an organization. All the other components discussed in Steps 1 to 6 will most certainly have an effect on the quality of the product itself, the results obtained and how these are received by the end-users, but these components alone will not guarantee a successful end result. The action planning and utilization process is the key to creating any type of significant impact in the way things are done in the organization. Figure 7.1 presents a graphic depiction of the change in emphasis at this final stage between the more tactical aspects of the survey

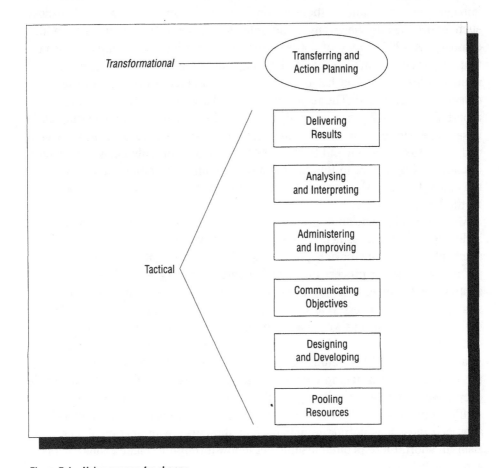

Figure 7.1   Using surveys for change

process and organizational transformation. Even if the construction, administration, communication, analysis and delivery are conducted with the utmost of competence, if the survey results are not absorbed and ultimately used by organizational members to make key decisions the survey cannot be considered to have been *maximally* effective. Regardless of the goals and objectives of the assessment itself (e.g., to measure attitudes and perceptions, to track managerial behaviours, to identify areas for change and development), it is of paramount importance that managers and employees take ownership of the findings and make changes happen as a result. A survey might be intended primarily to take an assessment of the general morale of employees, but if the information obtained is not used in some manner (e.g., from communicating to employees that people are generally positive about working for the organization, to there are significant issues and concerns that need to be dealt with) it cannot have much of an effect. This may be an acceptable outcome for some practitioners and some survey sponsors as well; however, it is our position that this type of effort – i.e., where there is no clear intention of taking action based on survey results – should probably be avoided whenever possible. These situations often lead to apathy, frustration and negative energy on the part of the survey respondents and likely to damage the credibility of the survey sponsor and all who are involved in the effort. If someone is going to spend a significant amount of time, money and energy on a well constructed and implemented survey effort and expects employees to take time out from their busy work schedule to respond, then it is only fair that the results obtained should be used for some type of decision-making and/or organizational change. The purpose of this step is to discuss some of the most important issues and applications involved in this final, and often neglected, stage in the survey process.

BARRIERS TO THE TRANSFER OF OWNERSHIP

It is certainly no secret to the experienced survey practitioner that surveys are often a source of significant anxiety and trepidation for end-users (e.g., your 'clients', such as the survey sponsor, survey champion, key senior management members or other professionals such as those in HRD or OD functions). As the time of disclosure and reporting draws near, the end-user or client in question often may become reluctant to 'embrace' or own his or her data. This is due to the less than stellar findings on some if not many areas or variables measured by the survey instrument. When the ethics and integrity of senior leaders receive the lowest ratings overall from employees, for example, it can be difficult giving this feedback to the very same executives who were rated poorly at the start of the roll-out process.

Some organizations conduct employee opinion surveys annually as a part of their ongoing human resource and/or organization development strategy, but in many cases surveys are undertaken for diagnostic purposes by organizations that are experiencing significant problems or changes. These latter companies will look for an outside or external survey provider to help them design, administer, analyse and report the survey results. When this process has been well thought-out, co-ordinated and implemented it can flow amazingly smoothly. Even seasoned survey professionals, however, can have trouble in the final phases of reporting and action planning. This is when the proverbial 'rubber meets the road' and often the end-users of the survey results are not ready, willing or able to deal with the ramifications of less than favourable findings.

Needless to say, this is a very important time in the survey process that must be handled with a mixture of sensitivity and assertiveness on the part of the consultant or survey practitioner. Remember that the level of interest in the results tends to vary considerably with the amount of time taken by the survey team to communicate the findings. Timing is important during this final stage as well. At this juncture, the survey practitioner must be especially sensitive to the anxieties and fears of the client or end-user while at the same time guiding the survey sponsor through the process of disseminating information and action planning in a timely manner. It is at this phase in the survey cycle that some of the most reasonable and sensible end-users and/or survey sponsors can be blinded by their own fears and rendered virtually unwilling and/or incapable of taking action. There are many ways in which this anxiety can manifest itself; for the purposes of this step we will limit our discussion to the following two forms we have experienced most frequently: paralysis and denial.

The first mechanism for the expression of anxiety comes from a term coined by one of our professors in graduate school who was an experienced consultant and survey practitioner. What he affectionately called 'analysis paralysis' refers to a person's inability to get beyond the analysis stage (Step 5) when working with survey data. If you are struggling with a survey sponsor to put the finishing touches on a survey report that you have been toiling over with gruelling effort for weeks, and have gone through endless iterations of edits and your client keeps asking you for 'one more set of analyses, just to be sure we have got it all right', then you probably are on the receiving end of an analysis paralysis situation.

However, this may not be serious. Often in these cases, if your client is at all reasonable, some simple nudging will suffice. Gently, let your client know that what he or she is experiencing is normal but counterproductive. Remind him or her of your original agreements regarding content and delivery timetables. Point out the implicit agreement with the survey respondents to provide a valid and legitimate set of results. Be supportive of your client and walk him or her through the issues. It is at this point in the survey process that you will have to be acutely aware of your client's emotional and psychological states *vis-à-vis* the survey effort. Be patient and remember that even though you may have seen this paralysis happen many times before, your client probably has not. If all else fails, use the data to help your client move beyond his or her anxieties. In most cases there will be ample write-in commentary expounding on the necessity to report out results to all involved and take action. Sometimes the words of co-workers can be more convincing than any argument made by the survey practitioner or survey team.

Another possible manifestation of anxiety that may not be so benign is that of outright denial of the results. This is a very convenient defence mechanism, for if the client rejects the findings of the survey then he or she does not have to do anything (i.e., take any actions) about them. If not rectified, this is something that can render your survey useless. Denial can take several forms:

1. Flat rejection of the survey findings (e.g., 'these data are inaccurate', 'people didn't understand the question', 'people didn't understand the scales', 'this is not what's really going on here', etc.).
2. Placing blame and/or finding fault with the survey team and/or process ('your sample is bad', 'you didn't ask the right questions', 'you surveyed people at wrong time', etc.).
3. Requests for additional external points of comparison (e.g., usually those that are intended to be used to demonstrate that the organization is not doing that poorly after all).
4. Attempts to whitewash the data (e.g., completely taking control of and rewriting the survey findings to the point where the 'official' communication of the results to others are obtuse and/or totally inaccurate).

Of these forms of denial, the fourth is the most serious, and although this does not occur all that often, it is an unpleasant reality of the survey process, particularly for those who have invested significantly in the effort.

As with paralysis, denial can be overcome but requires some skill and shrewdness on the part of the survey practitioner or team. Experience tells us that reporting the results of a survey can be fraught with political complications, which are veritable landmines to the transfer and action planning processes. Denial often occurs as a result of the sponsor's or senior management's fear of delivering bad news to the organization. It often seems as if the end-user is blaming the survey team for the content and issues identified in the results themselves. Despite conventional wisdom, the messenger often does get shot. If you find yourself on the receiving end of a denial situation it is often due to a combination of (a) this very rational fear or concern of exposure in conjunction with (b) the fact the client does not feel adequate ownership of the survey process, which in turn is often due to a lack of involvement in the process from the beginning. As a survey practitioner, it is your job at this point to facilitate and engender a sense of ownership in the data in order to transfer the results to action on the part of the end-user. This is not an easy task at the eleventh hour, especially if you are asking the client to own something that is not particularly that positive (and most surveys do have their share of positives and negatives). Nevertheless, if this denial is not overcome, you can go no further with the results however wonderfully analysed and prepared they may be. There are several actions that can be taken to avert this problem:

1. Keep the key end-users (e.g., the survey sponsor and/or senior management members) fully briefed during all phases of the survey process. If this is not possible, work very closely with the appropriate staff members to ensure joint ownership. The goal here is to pass the baton.
2. Encourage the client to put his or her signature on as many documents and memos as possible regarding the survey process (both before and after administration).
3. Have the survey sponsor commit to reporting the results (in a way that he or she is comfortable with) to everyone who participated in the survey process.
4. Arrange for the survey sponsor to commit, in advance of the administration, to an action plan.
5. Go back to the original contract, remind the sponsor of his or her commitment to action. And finally,
6. Don't give up!

In the end it is your job to help your client see the light at the end of the tunnel.

A COMMITMENT TO ACTION

As mentioned above, one of the first and most important elements in ensuring that a survey effort will result in organizational change is a commitment to action on the part of the survey champion, client and/or the senior management of the organization. Just as a highly visible, active and respected promoter of the survey effort is very important at the beginning of the process when laying the groundwork for organizational participation and commitment (as discussed in Step 1), so too is this role immensely important before, during and after the delivery and communication of the findings throughout the organization. Having the support of senior individuals lends credibility and importance to survey results that otherwise simply would not be there. With the plethora of information and inputs coming into people's lives on a daily basis, survey findings are

Table 7.1 Sample chief executive officer communication regarding survey results

---

Dear Colleague,

We are constantly striving to become a better organization – more productive, profitable, service oriented and better managed. The latter includes being more attuned and responsive to your needs. This is why we chose to examine the way we run our organization by conducting an organization survey. During the past two months we asked every company XYZ employee to take part in our first organization-wide survey. We wanted to know what you think of XYZ as a place to work as well as your views about our future direction, the way we manage and how you regard your job and working environment.

We were very pleased that over 5,000 company XYZ employees completed the survey process. As a result we now have a great deal of useful information that we will use to improve XYZ. Your responses show areas where we are strong as well as those we need to improve. This report contains a summary and analysis, followed by a full and detailed presentation of all the results. Some of these results may be surprising or may confirm what you already knew. In any case, as you read through the report, I expect you will get a better view of XYZ, as I have.

By raising our own awareness of the issues that influence our performance, I believe we are taking an important step. Starting now we will explore these results and together develop a series of actions to address your needs and concerns.

In the weeks and months ahead, I hope that you and your managers will be discussing how this can be accomplished. We will report to you on survey-related actions by a special newsletter. I hope all of you will take an active role in using the survey results. Finally, I wish to thank all of you for your participation and therefore invaluable contribution to XYZ.

Jane Doe

CEO Company XYZ

---

likely to be treated as another distraction that is not particularly (or seemingly) related to one's day-to-day job if they are not associated with positive change by someone of stature. A commitment to action, often expressed in terms of the survey champion's own reaction and response to the results obtained, is key to building energy among others to use the results in their own decision-making processes.

The example in Table 7.1 demonstrates one way to obtain senior leadership's stamp of approval. A letter or memo of this type is frequently included as the introduction to survey findings and sets the stage for action planning. Written communications alone are not sufficient to create the energy needed for successful change as a result of a survey but they are important and set the tone for future communications, particularly when written and signed by the CEO or another highly visible figure.

CASCADING RESULTS AND ACTION PLANNING

The cascading method of delivery is another means of promoting a higher level of commitment to action in the organization, particularly where significant portions of management's time is used to discuss the survey results obtained. These types of working sessions, if facilitated correctly, convey to the rest of the organization that the survey process is indeed (a) worth the effort, (b) being taken seriously by management, and (c) going to result in some tangible outcomes

Often complex and laborious, the cascading process is invaluable in obtaining the level of commitment necessary for success in the action planning phase. This type of top-down approach is aimed at getting the support of senior leadership and key players in the organization very early on in the reporting process. By using this method of delivering the results the survey practitioner or team is able to obtain the commitment of the survey sponsor and senior leadership and, perhaps, some initial actions undertaken before most organization members are even aware that the survey analysis process has been completed. This provides the practitioner with a much needed headstart.

Reporting of results starts with a series of meetings with the survey sponsor to inform him or her of the main findings from the survey (see Step 6 for additional information about this process). Some type of executive summary is usually reported at this time. The purpose of this meeting is twofold:

1. To provide the immediate client (e.g., the survey sponsor or perhaps the survey champion) with the imminent findings before the rest of the organization (including the rest of senior leadership) has a chance to see them.
2. To allay any last-minute fears or anxieties about what to expect after the results have been released.

These preliminary meetings are not only held as a matter of courtesy to the primary survey client, but also to manage the process and flow of information as well as his or her concerns while reaffirming the importance of a sincere commitment to action. Given the level of anxiety that is often present, the importance of this meeting or series of meetings cannot be overemphasized.

Regardless of how this commitment to action is communicated, remember that surveys raise employees' awareness of issues and, likewise, their expectations. If management refuses to acknowledge or address these factors, frustration and apathy are likely consequences. In some cases conditions such as morale can get worse when a survey effort is ignored or buried. A formal and tangible management response is an important factor in determining the success or failure of a survey effort. This response usually consists of the following five elements:

1. Considerable thought and discussion about what the survey results mean.
2. Careful determination of how the survey results should be communicated to others.
3. Planning for what actions should be taken.
4. Taking action.
5. Following up on the success or failure of your actions.

THE ACTION PLANNING PROCESS

We have recommended throughout that for a survey effort to be considered effective it should, at the very least, contribute to important decision-making processes and/or result in a series of actions; however, we have yet to describe specifically how this works and what these types of actions and outcomes might be. The identification and selection of possible alternatives following a survey effort are driven largely by the outcome of the data analysis and interpretation phase. As discussed in Step 5, the use of conceptual models, theoretical frameworks, trends, grouping analyses and/or other types of corporate directives (e.g., vision, values, competencies, strategic directives, etc.) can be very useful in providing a view of the bigger picture and where efforts for change might be best directed. If, for example, the analyses indicate that ratings of employee satisfaction are highly related to perceptions regarding the poor state of the management information systems currently in use, then it is clear that management needs to make changes to these systems. This might mean updating the system itself, replacing it with an entirely new one, or providing more training on how to maximize the use of the system currently in place. Whatever the outcome, management almost always needs to proceed through the following steps:

1. Recognize that this is a problem and that it has consequences.
2. Show their recognition to employees through some form of communication.
3. Prepare a plan for improving or replacing the technology employed.
4. Make a commitment to acting on this plan.

If the content analysis and interpretation of the write-in comments indicate a significant lack of management emphasis on developing employees and preparing them for the future, then this is an area that probably needs to be addressed as well. Depending on the situation, however, the required response might be anywhere from ensuring that all available developmental opportunities are effectively communicated to employees as they become available, to designing an entirely new training and development system aimed at giving managers the appropriate skills to train and mentor their direct employees.

Besides the use of larger, more complex frameworks and models, some

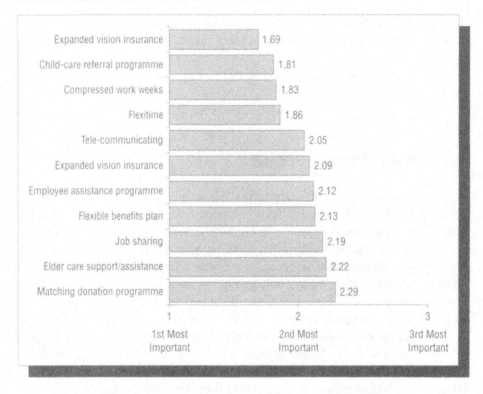

Figure 7.2   Mean ranking of most important employee benefits

survey questionnaires have their own action planning prioritization process built into the items themselves. For example, based on a mean ranking of what employees consider to be their most important benefits (as described in Figure 7.2), it would be relatively easy to determine what types of follow-up interventions should be made regarding addition or modification of an existing benefits plan in an organization. If the data analysis and interpretation have been completed with an attention to detail and the involvement of other key players and constituents in the organization, the types of outcomes and actions necessary should be relatively easy to determine.

Specifying the types of outcomes, interventions and actions that might result from a large-scale survey effort would be never-ending. Just as the content of the data itself can reflect issues at the work unit, department or organizational level, so too can the interventions and actions taken as a result of the analysis process be directed at different levels where appropriate (see Figure 7.3). In this way, multiple interventions can be used concurrently to achieve a greater and more integrated level of impact. For example, a possible *intervention at the individual*

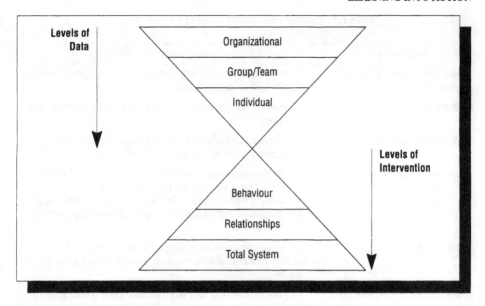

Figure 7.3   Levels of data and intervention

level directed at changing managerial behaviours might consist of a multi-rater (360-degree) feedback initiative. Similarly, at the relationship level, group on group feedback might be appropriate or perhaps team-building efforts and the introduction of cross-functional task forces designed to integrate roles and responsibilities across groups. Interventions directed at achieving a total systems-level change in the organization might consist of a multitude of co-ordinated efforts across different areas (e.g., restructuring, changing reward and benefit systems, new leadership, culture change).

The only real constraints are those existing in the quality and quantity of the data obtained. It would probably not make sense to pursue a restructuring effort based on recommendations from a survey effort for a large department where the responses obtained were not based on a random sample and reflected only 15 per cent of the total number of employees in that area. If, on the other hand, 80 per cent of employees agreed that the current structure is dysfunctional and creates conflict and inefficiencies, then some set of changes in this regard might be warranted. This is one of the reasons why an effective and successful survey effort is more than just a simple series of questions (and the reason for the exist-ence of this book and others like it). You know what they say: 'Garbage in – garbage out'.

While certainly not exhaustive, Table 7.2 provides a sampling of some of the major types of interventions and follow-up actions that can result from a

Table 7.2   Potential interventions following a survey effort

Intervention	Issues intended to address
Assessment centres/training needs assessment	To assess employee (typically managers') skill levels in key areas to identify specific training needs.
Skills training	To provide employees with the requisite skills to perform their jobs effectively.
Team-building sessions	Opportunities for teams and/or work groups to enhance group processes, working and interpersonal relationships.
Leadership development	To identify and develop leaders within the organization. To orient current and potential leaders to the values and performance standards of the organization. To provide a venue for networking and relationship-building among leaders in different organizational functions or units.
Restructuring	To reapportion resources according to need and business performance in an effort to maximize productivity and minimize waste.
Business process re-engineering	To work 'smarter' and more efficiently with existing resources. To maximize performance and streamline existing ways of doing things.
Multi-rater (360-degree) feedback	To create self-awareness among leaders and managers through the process of giving and receiving feedback. To provide a unit of measurement on which leaders and managers can measure their performance and the accomplishment of goals and objectives. Culture change through common practices.

large-scale survey effort and the types of issues these are typically intended to address. Those interested in finding out more about specific interventions as well as additional options should look to the organization development and change management literatures (e.g., Beckhard and Pritchard, 1992; Berger, Sikora and Berger, 1994; Burke, 1994; Church and Waclawski, 1997; Hornstein et al., 1971; Howard, 1994; Kanter, Stein and Jick, 1992; Tichy, 1983).

In some cases, particularly when working at lower levels in the organization, it can be beneficial for the end-users to identify and work through the specific issues in their data themselves or in conjunction with a survey consultant rather than identify these issues up front. As discussed in Step 6, this process of collaboration can lead to greater levels of commitment regarding intended outcomes as well as greater specificity in the types of interventions identified and ultimately implemented. Table 7.3 is a sample step-by-step set of instructions and accompanying worksheets that can be used to help people work through their specific survey-related issues. Of course, the implementation of this approach to using and working with survey results needs to have been decided long before the questionnaire is administered. Once again, this brings us back to one of the issues (discussed in Step 1) behind putting in place a thorough survey plan and concrete objectives established at the outset of the survey process. If the survey practitioner and sponsor know how deep in the organization and to what ends the data will be delivered (e.g., senior management only for general trend analysis versus work group levels for every manager with 15 or more direct reports), the appropriate individuals can be involved and the right demographic information needed for cutting the data included in the instrument. Once the data have been collected, however, and even if managers are ready and willing to use their individual results, if the demographic information was not included it is probably impossible to obtain the results needed for effective action planning at this level.

LINKING SURVEY RESULTS TO OTHER MEASURES OF PERFORMANCE

The administration of organization assessment surveys has become an increasingly important and popular part of many organization and human resource development and change efforts. Surveys can be particularly useful when their results are linked to other measures of organizational performance (e.g., customer service ratings, financial performance indicators, measures of turnover and attrition, etc.). Linking survey results to these hard measures enables organizations to identify relationships between various aspects of organizational functioning (i.e., leadership, company values, management practices, policies and procedures etc.) and desired performance outcomes. Figure 7.4 provides an example of how various issues and item related content areas might be linked to hard performance indicators. In this way survey results can be used to target areas for change which will enhance organizational effectiveness as well as demonstrating the importance and relevance of survey findings to people's day-to-day work activities. Not surprisingly, there is a plethora of issues to consider in linking survey results to other measures of performance. These can be broken down into three broad categories: theoretical, political and technical.

Regarding theoretical considerations, the main objective here is to determine relevant indices of comparison. For example, deciding to link a survey which measures managers' opinions about the company's dental plan to ratings of external customer service does not make sense. Why would anyone expect satisfaction solely with a dental plan to translate directly to the quality of customer service provided? The nature of managerial behaviours in the work group, however, is quite likely to have an impact in this regard. In determining linking variables one must identify the appropriate measures of performance that can be logically and empirically merged with the survey data. This will necessitate at the very least a thorough review of relevant literature regarding the variables to

171

Table 7.3   Sample survey worksheets and action planning guide

---

DEVELOPING ACTION PLANS

1. *Move from your reactions to the data to next steps*

   Meet with your team and go over the results of the survey. Discuss how you will use the data to improve what you do and how you will do it. What might be some areas you want to work through as a team?

   The following worksheets provide a place for you to record what you have learned from the survey. Use the first worksheet to identify areas of strength and those that need improvement. Then use the second worksheet to summarize in 3–5 points the most important issues for your team to work on. What did you learn and what do you need to work on as a result?

Areas of strength	*Areas for improvement*
Communicating with direct reports	Confronting my superiors when necessary
Giving my direct reports timely feedback	Fostering communication between my department and others
Rewarding and recognizing high performers	Providing a clear direction for my department

---

Most important issues

---

1. As a team, we need to integrate our work processes with other departments in company XYZ
2. As a team, we need to determine our future direction and objectives
3. As a leader, I need to challenge my supervisors when appropriate instead of being silent
4. As a leader, I need to provide strong leadership and help my team reach its objectives
5. As a leader, I need to take a more hands on approach to management

---

2. *Establish a contract for working on the data*

   Set up a timeline of activities and decide who will do what. Schedule your next meeting to communicate expectations for what each member will bring to the next meeting.

Contract to my team

As our team leader, I promise to actively work on addressing the key issues for our team that resulted from the Company XYZ survey. I promise to hold monthly meetings to review our objectives and progress on these issues. Also, I promise to be open and receptive to honest feedback regarding our progress.

---

3. *Check your group process*

   End your meeting with a check on the group's process. How did the meeting go? What went well and what didn't go well? How can you do things differently in the future? Make sure that everyone understands the main issues, is comfortable with plans you developed to address these issues and is clear about his or her responsibility in the change process.

4. *Follow up on your commitments*

   Measure the success or failure of your efforts by setting systems in place to evaluate progress. This can occur through group discussions or resurveying on key issues.

Table 7.3   continued

5. *Conduct periodic meetings to evaluate your team's progress*
    These follow-up meetings can be incorporated into your staff meetings or can occur independently. Whatever the case, these meetings should occur frequently and on a regular basis to ensure maximum commitment to the change process.

The following worksheet can be used as a starting point for recording your team's action plans and charting your progress.

Issue	*Point person*	*Intervention*	*Deadline*	*Results expected*
Intergroup relations	Mai Reeport	Team building exercise and work sharing programme	9/9/99	Elimination of duplication of effort, better relationships outside our department
Challenging up	Jane Manager	Regular meeting with my supervisor to discuss key issues	9/9/99	Voicing issues of my department to leadership
Setting direction	Jane Manager and all team members	Department mission statement with specific objectives and timelines	9/9/99	Gaining clarity about where we are going and why Alignment with corporate strategy

be linked and a solid research design. Organizations that plan on linking variables to survey data will be best served by considering these types of issues in advance of the survey design. Such consideration and planning will allow specific issues and complexities related to the research questions of interest to be built into the survey process a priori.

Considering the possible political implications and/or 'true availability' of linking survey data to hard performance measures is also advisable. Many people would perceive the need to work the political process in this regard as a necessary evil, as we have discussed throughout this book; however, aligning rather than alienating key players in the organization is essential to the success of any survey-related effort. For example, if the results of a survey effort are intended to be linked to individual or departmental performance measures (e.g., sales, revenue, customer satisfaction, repeat business, etc.), going through the

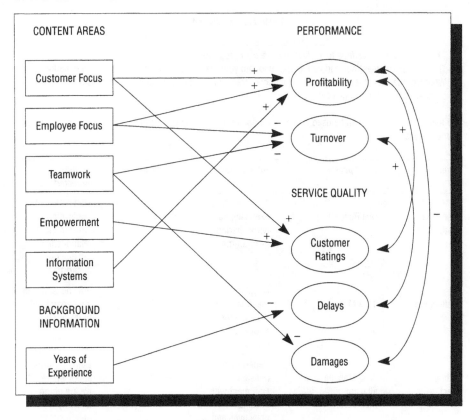

Figure 7.4 Linking survey results to performance measures
Reproduced by permission: MCB University Press

proper channels to obtain the necessary data and explaining its uses will be of paramount importance. The last thing the survey team wants to do is alienate respondents by overburdening them in this process. Further, if the data are obtained through inappropriate means the resulting chaos and backlash when discovered could easily destroy the perceived integrity and validity of the survey data. It is an unfortunate fact, and we have seen this happen often enough in practice, that other individuals in the organization not directly involved in (or controlling) the survey process may not be interested in sharing their data with another professional, regardless of the intended uses and potential benefits of the information that might be obtained. These types of situations make the process of linking survey data to other measures seem almost impossible at times.

A consideration of technical computability is also required. In order to link to other measures the survey results obtained, it is imperative to ensure that the level of analysis between the various datasets is consistent. Again, this is an issue to consider during the planning and design phase of the survey effort if, indeed, this type of additional analysis is of significant interest. The appropriate demographic or background variables must be included in the instrument from the start to provide the opportunity for adequate level-matching among datasets. For example, if the desire is to link external customer service ratings collected at the department level to ratings of empowerment obtained from a survey effort at the department level, then the practitioner needs to make sure that the survey data will (a) include this variable with the same departmental categories, and (b) that the data will be capable of being averaged and subsequently analysed at this level as well. The analyses that can be conducted will ultimately be limited by the greatest level of specificity of the data collected on both measures (i.e., the lowest available point). So going back to our previous example, if either of the measures to be linked is not specific enough (e.g., the data have been collected at the divisional but not the departmental levels), the specificity of the analyses will be hampered. Other technical considerations include the ability to link databases, which will necessitate the use of compatible statistical packages and/or spreadsheets. Although not insurmountable, linking different datasets can be complex and very time-consuming. Again, the advice or consultation of an experienced data analyst is invaluable here.

BUILDING SYSTEMS FOR EVALUATING SUCCESS

Measuring the progress of survey efforts is an important part of demonstrating commitment to the survey and also assuring that things are in fact changing for the better. Informal, 'how are we doing' conversations and meetings are useful in gauging a department's or organization's progress, but these are not enough. Serious evaluation must be undertaken to solidify commitment and to ensure continued efforts in the right direction. Many organizational surveys and, subsequently, survey-related interventions are implemented in the context of ongoing organizational change and/or development initiatives, and it may be difficult to parse out the effects of such interventions. Nevertheless, without such attempts, proof of change and the importance of surveying in general will be lacking.

One of the main difficulties in evaluating the success of any organizational survey effort is that a valid and reliable instrument itself is necessary but not sufficient for affecting change. As we have discussed above, there are many factors involved in creating meaningful organizational change through surveys, not all of which are under any one individual's or group's control, including the survey practitioner or at times even the survey sponsor. For evaluation purposes, however, it can be a difficult task to determine exactly which was the principal factor in causing the success or downfall of any given set of interventions following a survey effort. One method that can be helpful for examining the effectiveness of a series of interventions is to use comparative groups. This process involves finding a group of different departments, functions, regions or work groups in the same organization that went about the communication and use of their specific results by means of significantly different methods. Some groups, for example, may have provided more general communication of the findings; others may have delivered the results to every manager and had them work through the findings with their teams. Since these quasi-experimental groups would typically share the same organizational culture, the survey practitioner is likely to find useful insights into the process of working with utilizing survey data in their particular organization. These insights, then, may also be applicable to other troubled areas and/or future survey efforts.

One final note: the evaluation of interventions aimed at organization development and change (such as organizational surveys) is historically weak. In fact, the research methods employed in past evaluations of OD and HRD related interventions have recently come under serious scrutiny (Ledford and Mohrman, 1993; Roberts and Robertson, 1993; Robertson, Roberts and Porras, 1993; Terpstra, 1981). More specifically, researchers have found evidence of a negative relationship between the methodological rigour of evaluations of these types of interventions and their reported success (Golembiewski and Sun, 1990; Roberts and Robertson, 1993; Terpstra, 1981). Known as *positive-findings bias*, this disturbing relationship has been hypothesized to stem from the evaluator's unconscious desire to prove the efficacy of his or her interventions (Terpstra, 1981). This finding can have serious implications for the survey practitioner who wishes to evaluate interventions which arise from his or her own survey findings. Therefore, it is probably better to work with an objective third party who can help devise an impartial way of measuring progress. Some of the most common and useful ways of measuring progress are (a) resurveying at a later date, (b) conducting focus groups and/or interviews to assess change, and (c) measuring changes in absenteeism, turnover and productivity rates. In the end, however, it is often the survey sponsor, champion and, indeed, the entire client organization who decide if the effort was in fact a success.

CHECKLIST FOR STEP 7

1. Minimize barriers to the transfer of ownership.
   Be sensitive to the anxieties of the client while guiding them through the process of disseminating information and action planning.
   - Work with the client to get beyond 'analysis paralysis' when analysing results. Help them visualize the finished product and commit to hard deadlines for roll-out.

- Minimize possible causes for denial by keeping key end-users fully briefed during the survey process, and getting the client to commit to reporting the results.

2. Get a commitment to action.
   - Start by meeting with the survey sponsor to inform him or her of the main findings from the survey.
   - Then, set a process in place for a formal and tangible management response which helps the client (a) discuss what the survey results mean, (b) determine how the survey results should be communicated, (c) plan for what actions should be taken, (d) take action, and (e) follow up on the success or failure of actions taken.

3. Begin the action planning process.
   - Help the individual end-user (a) recognize there is a problem and that it has consequences, (b) show their recognition of this to employees through communication, (c) prepare a plan for improvement, and (d) make a commitment to acting on this plan.

4. Link survey results to other measures of performance.
   - Target areas for change which will enhance organizational effectiveness such as productivity, sales, quality measures, customer satisfaction, etc.

5. Build systems for measuring progress and evaluating success.
   - Get client organization to record actions taken as a result of the survey and to measure the impact of actions taken.
   - Contract with client to resurvey six months to one year later.
   - Help client set up an internal survey process for long-term data collection and measurement of results.

References

Adams, S. (1996), *The Dilbert Principle*, New York: Harper Business.

Atwater, L. E., and Yammarino, F. J. (1992), 'Does Self–Other Agreement on Leadership Perceptions Moderate the Validity of Leadership and Performance Predictions?', *Personnel Psychology*, **45**, 141–64.

Babbie, R. E. (1973), *Survey Research Methods*, Belmont, CA: Wadsworth Publishing.

Bauman, R. P., Jackson, P., and Lawrence, J. T. (1997), *From Promise to Performance: A journey of transformation at SmithKline Beecham*, Boston: Harvard Business School Press.

Beckhard, R., and Harris, R. T. (1987), *Organizational Transitions: Managing Complex Change*, 2nd edn, Reading, MA: Addison-Wesley.

Beckhard, R., and Pritchard, W. (1992), *Changing the Essence: the Art of Creating and Leading Fundamental Change in Organizations*, San Francisco: Jossey-Bass.

Berger, L. A., Sikora, M. J., and Berger, D. R. (eds) (1994), *The Change Management Handbook: a Road Map to Corporate Transformation*, Burr Ridge, IL: Irwin.

Berk, R. A. (1983), 'Applications of the General Linear Model to Survey Data', in P. H. Rossi, J. D. Wright and A. B. Anderson (eds), *The Handbook of Survey Research*, San Diego, CA: Academic Press, pp. 495–546.

Block, P. (1981), *Flawless Consulting: a Guide to Getting your Expertise Used*, San Diego, CA: University Associates.

Breisch, R. E. (1996), 'Are You Listening?', *Quality Progress*, **29**(1), 59–62.

Bunker, B. B., and Alban, B. T. (1997), *Large Group Interventions: Engaging the Whole System for Rapid Change*, San Francisco: Jossey-Bass.

Burke, W. W. (1994), *Organization Development: a Process of Learning and Changing*, 2nd edn, Reading, MA: Addison-Wesley.

Burke, W. W., Coruzzi, C. A., and Church, A. H. (1996), 'The Organizational Survey as an Intervention for Change', in A. I. Kraut (ed.), *Organizational Surveys: Tools for Assessment and Change*, San Francisco: Jossey-Bass, pp. 41–66.

Burke, W. W., and Jackson, P. (1991), 'Making the SmithKline Beecham Merger Work', *Human Resource Management*, **30**, 69–87.

Burke, W. W., and Litwin, G. H. (1992), 'A Causal Model of Organizational Performance and Change', *Journal of Management*, **18**, 523–45.

Camp, R. C. (1995), *Business Process Benchmarking: Finding and Implementing Best Practices*, Milwaukee, WI: ASQC Quality Press.

Church, A. H. (1993), 'Estimating the Effect of Incentives on Mail Survey Response Rates: a Meta-analysis', *Public Opinion Quarterly*, **57**(1), 62–79.

Church, A. H. (1994a), 'Managerial Self-awareness in High Performing Individuals in Organizations' doctoral dissertation, Columbia University, *Dissertation Abstracts International*, *55-05B*, 2028.

Church, A. H. (1994b), 'The Character of Organizational Communication: a Review and New Conceptualization', *International Journal of Organizational Analysis*, **2**(1), 18–53.

179

Church, A. H. (1996), 'Giving your Organizational Communication C-P-R', *Leadership and Organizational Development Journal*, 17(7), 4–11.

Church, A. H. (1997), 'Managerial Self-awareness in High Performing Individuals in Organizations', *Journal of Applied Psychology*, 82(2), 281–92.

Church, A. H., and Bracken, D. W. (1997), 'Advancing the State of the Art of 360-degree Feedback: Special Issue Editors' Comments on the Research and Practice of Multirater Assessment Methods', *Group and Organization Management*, 22(2), 149–61.

Church, A. H., Margiloff, A., and Coruzzi, C. A. (1995), 'Using Surveys for Change: an Applied Example in a Pharmaceuticals Organization', *Leadership and Organization Development Journal*, 16(4), 3–11.

Church, A. H. and Waclawski, J. (1997), 'Multi-rater Degree Feedback Systems: How to Make Them Work', *Quality Progress*, in press.

Edwards, J. E., Thomas, M. D., Rosenfeld, P., and Booth-Kewley, S. (1997), *How to Conduct Organizational Surveys: a Step-by-step Guide*, Thousand Oaks, CA: Sage.

Fink, A. (1995), *The Survey Handbook*, Thousand Oaks, CA: Sage.

Frankel, M. (1983), 'Sampling Theory', in P. H. Rossi, J. D. Wright and A. B. Anderson (eds), *The Handbook of Survey Research*, San Diego, CA: Academic Press, pp. 21–67.

Golembiewski, R. T., and Sun, B. C. (1990), 'Positive Findings Bias in QWL Studies: Rigor and Outcomes in a Large Sample', *Journal of Management*, 16, 665–74.

Higgs, A. C., and Ashworth, S. D. (1996), 'Organizational Surveys: Tools for Assessment and Research', in A. I. Kraut (ed.), *Organizational Surveys: Tools for Assessment and Change*, San Francisco: Jossey-Bass, pp. 19–40.

Hornstein, H. A., Bunker, B. B., Burke, W. W., Gindes, M., and Lewicki, R. J. (eds), (1971), *Social Intervention: a Behavioral Science Approach*, New York: Free Press.

Howard, A. and Associates (eds) (1994), *Diagnosis for Organizational Change: Methods and Models*, New York: Guilford Press.

Howard, A. H. (1994), *Diagnosis for Organizational Change: Methods and Models*, New York: Guilford Press.

Johnson, R. H. (1996), 'Life in the Consortium: the Mayflower Group', in A. I. Kraut (ed.), *Organizational Surveys: Tools for Assessment and Change*, San Francisco: Jossey-Bass, pp. 285–309.

Jones, J. E., and Bearley, W. K. (1995), *Surveying Employees: a Practical Guidebook*, Amherst, MA: HRD Press.

Kanter, P. M., Stein, R. A., and Jick, T. D. (1992), *The Challenge of Organizational Change: How Companies Experience It and Leaders Guide It*, New York: Free Press.

Katz, D., and Kahn, R. L. (1978), *The Social Psychology of Organizations*, 2nd edn, New York: John Wiley.

Kotter, J. P. (1995), 'Leading Change: Why Transformation Efforts Fail', *Harvard Business Review*, 73(2), 59–67.

Kraut, A. I. (1996a), 'An Overview of Organizational Surveys', in A. I. Kraut (ed.), *Organizational Surveys: Tools for Assessment and Change*, San Francisco: Jossey-Bass, pp. 1–14.

Kraut, A. I. (1996b), 'Planning and Conducting the Survey: Keeping the Strategic Purpose in Mind', in A. I. Kraut (ed.), *Organizational Surveys: Tools for Assessment and Change*, San Francisco: Jossey-Bass, pp. 149–76.

Kuhnert, K., and McCauley, D. P. (1996), 'Applying Alternative Survey Methods', in A. I. Kraut (ed.), *Organizational Surveys: Tools for Assessment and Change*, San Francisco: Jossey-Bass, pp. 233–54.

Ledford, G. E. jr and Mohrman, S. A. (1993), 'Self-design for High Involvement: a Large-scale Organizational Change', *Human Relations*, 46(1), 143–73.

Lewin, K. (1958), 'Group Decision and Social Change', in E. E. Maccoby, T. M. Newcomb and E. L. Hartley (eds), *Readings in Social Psychology*, New York: Holt, Rinehart and Winston, pp. 197–211.

Nadler, D. A. (1977), *Feedback and Organization Development: Using Data-based Methods*, Reading, MA: Addison-Wesley.

Nadler, D. A., and Tushman, M. L. (1992), 'Designing Organizations that Have Good Fit: a Framework for Understanding New Architectures', in D. A. Nadler, M. S. Gerstein, R. B. Shaw, and associates (eds), *Organizational Architecture: Designs for Changing Organizations*, San Francisco: Jossey-Bass, pp. 39–59.

Paul, K. B., and Bracken, D. W. (1995), 'Everything You Always Wanted to Know about Employee Surveys', *Training and Development*, 49(1), 45–9.

Pedhauzer, E. J. (1982), *Multiple Regression in Behavioral Research: Explanation and Prediction*, 2nd edn, New York: Holt, Rinehart and Winston.

Rea, L. M., and Parker, R. A. (1992), *Designing and Conducting Survey Research: a Comprehensive Guide*, San Francisco: Jossey-Bass.

Rea, L. M., and Parker, R. A. (1997), *Designing and Conducting Survey Research: a Comprehensive Guide (2nd edn)*, San Francisco: Jossey-Bass.

Roberts, D. R., and Robertson, P. J. (1993), 'Positive-findings Bias, and Measuring Methodological Rigor, in Evaluations of Organization Development', *Journal of Applied Psychology*, 77(6), 918–25.

Robertson, P. J., Roberts, D. R., and Porras, J. I. (1993), 'Dynamics of Planned Organizational Change: Assessing Empirical Support for a Theoretical Model', *Academy of Management Journal*, 36(3), 619–34.

Rossi, P. H., Wright, J. D., and Anderson, A. B. (1983), 'Sample Surveys: History, Current Practice, and Future Prospects', in P. H. Rossi, J. D. Wright, and A. B. Anderson (eds), *The Handbook of Survey Research*, San Diego, CA: Academic Press, pp. 1–20.

Sashkin, M., and Kiser, K. J. (1993), *Putting Total Quality Management to Work*, San Francisco: Berrett-Koehler.

Schaffer, R. H., and Thomson, H. A. (1992), 'Successful Change Programs Begin with Results', *Harvard Business Review*, 70(1), 80–89.

Schein, E. H. (1988), *Process Consultation Volume 1: Its Role in Organizational Development (2nd edn)*, Reading, MA: Addison-Wesley.

Schumacker, R. E., and Lomax, R. G. (1996), *A Beginner's Guide to Structural Equation Modeling*, Mahwah, NJ: Lawrence Erlbaum.

Schuman, H., and Kalton, G. (1985), 'Survey Methods', in G. Lindzey, and E. Aronson (eds), *The Handbook of Social Psychology*, 3rd edn, vol. 1, New York: Random House, pp. 635–97.

Spector, B., and Beer, M. (1994), 'Beyond TQM Programmes', *Journal of Organizational Change Management*, 7(2), 63–70.

Spendolini, M. J. (1992), *The Benchmarking Book*, New York: AMACOM.

Stolzenberg, R. M., and Land, K. C. (1982), 'Causal Modeling and Survey Research', in P. H. Rossi, J. D. Wright and A. B. Anderson (eds), *The Handbook of Survey Research*, San Diego, CA: Academic Press, pp. 613–75.

Sudman, S. (1983), 'Applied Sampling', in P. H. Rossi, J. D. Wright, and A. B. Anderson (eds), *The Handbook of Survey Research*, San Diego, CA: Academic Press, pp. 145–94.

Tabachnick, B. G., and Fidell, L. S. (1989), *Using Multivariate Statistics*, 2nd edn, New York: Harper and Row.

Terpstra, D. E. (1981), 'Relationship between Methodological Rigor and Reported Outcomes in Organization Development Evaluation Research', *Journal of Applied Psychology*, 66, 541–3.

Tichy, N. M. (1983), *Managing Strategic Change: Technical, Political and Cultural Dynamics*, New York: John Wiley.

Trahant, B., and Burke, W. W. (1996), 'Creating a Change Reaction: How Understanding Organizational Dynamics Can Ease Reengineering', *National Productivity Review*, Autumn, 37–46.

Ulrich, D. (1997), *Human Resource Champions: the Next Agenda for Adding Value and Delivering Results*, Boston: Harvard Business School.

Van Velsor, E., Taylor, S., and Leslie, J. B. (1993), 'An Examination of the Relationships among Self-perception Accuracy, Self-awareness, Gender, and Leader Effectiveness', *Human Resource Management*, 32(2 and 3), 249–63.

Waclawski, J. (1996a), 'Using Organizational Survey Results to Improve Organizational Performance', *Managing Service Quality*, 6(4), 53–6.

Waclawski, J. (1996b), 'Large-scale Organizational Change and Organizational Performance', doctoral dissertation, Columbia University, *Dissertation Abstracts International, 57-05B,* 3443 (University Microfilms No. AAG9631797).

Weisbord, M. R. (1978), *Organizational Diagnosis: a Workbook of Theory and Practice,* Reading, MA: Addison-Wesley.

Weisbord, M. R. (1995), *Future Search: an Action Guide to Finding Common Ground in Organizations and Communities,* San Francisco: Berrett-Koehler.

Subject index

185

Index of authors cited